Stress Less Trust More

MEDITATIONS TO MANAGE STRESS AND ANXIETY

Rand Hummel

journeyforth®

Greenville, South Carolina

Library of Congress Cataloging-in Publication Data
Names: Hummel, Rand, 1956– author.
Title: Stress less—trust more : meditations to manage stress and anxiety /
    Rand Hummell.
Description: Greenville, South Carolina : JourneyForth, 2018.
Identifiers: LCCN 2018026952 (print) | LCCN 2018028684 (ebook) | ISBN
    9781628565614 (e-book) | ISBN 9781628565607 (pbk.)
Subjects: LCSH: Anxiety—Religious aspects—Christianity. | Stress
    management—Religious aspects—Christianity. | Trust in God—
    Christianity.
Classification: LCC BV4908.5 (ebook) | LCC BV4908.5 .H865 2018 (print)
    | DDC 242/.4—dc23
LC record available at https://lccn.loc.gov/2018026952

Design by Craig Oesterling
Page layout by Michael Boone

© 2018 BJU Press
Greenville, South Carolina 29609
JourneyForth Books is a division of BJU Press.

Printed in the United States of America
All rights reserved

ISBN 978-1-62856-560-7
eISBN 978-1-62856-561-4

15   14   13   12   11   10   9   8   7   6   5   4   3   2

Contents

Part One: What Does Christ Want Us to Know to Stress Less and Trust More?

Part Two: What Does Christ Ask Us to *Do* to Stress Less and Trust More?

Introduction

Stress, anxiety, and worry are all tyrants seeking to control our lives.

Life is stressful, and some stress is both serious and unavoidable, like the death of a loved one, divorce, cancer, a heart attack, or family members turning away from God. But there are other day-to-day stresses that cause us to focus on our discomforts and disappointments and keep our eyes off an all-providing, all-loving, exceedingly gracious God. It is these day-to-day stresses that are the focus of the thirty-one daily meditations in this small book.

The Lord understood and experienced more stress than we can ever imagine. It had to have been incredibly stressful for the Son of God to live on such a selfish, sinful, self-righteous earth.

When Christ said, "Take no thought," He meant it. One of the greatest messages ever preached—the

Sermon on the Mount—was preached by the greatest Teacher who ever lived—Jesus Christ. It remains the most powerful, life-transforming message in print today.

In a little fewer than 2,500 words, Jesus clearly described and defined the kind of character and attitude that He would love to bless and honor. He described character that does not stress out over every little issue and a kingdom-of-God attitude that comes directly from the heart and impacts the way we view God, ourselves, and others. It is an attitude that avoids stress and will permeate the kingdom of God forever and forever.

The stress-free attitude that Jesus the Messiah preached refuses to stop at religious externals or shallow commitment. It is not motivated by rich rewards or devastating consequences, but by a deep-seated love for Christ because of what He has done for us. What did He do? He did all that was necessary to remove our sin from us, reconcile us to God the Father, and adopt us as His own.

Now take a big breath before you meditate on each section of this little book and watch God give you a new insight on the stress in your life.

In Matthew 5, Christ told us what He wants us to *know* to lessen our stress. In Matthew 6–7, Christ told us what He wants us to *do* to lessen our stress. Listen carefully to Christ; learn from Him; obey Him; and enjoy the potential of living a life that manages stress in a Christ-honoring way.

In reality we are way too blessed to be stressed. We just don't realize it yet.

Stress less and trust more,
Rand

Too Blessed to Be Stressed

Take no *thought*.
Matthew 6:25, 31, 34; 10:19; Mark 13:11; Luke 12:22

Be *careful* [anxious] for nothing.
Philippians 4:6

Martha, Martha, thou art *careful* and troubled
about many things.
Luke 10:41

Anxiety attacks us when we least expect it. Where do you think most of your stress comes from? When are you most stressed? When are you least stressed? Are you more stressed at home or at work? Do you think it is possible for your stress to be significantly reduced or even eliminated?

Stressors vary. Stress levels differ in different seasons of life. What may stress you today may not stress you tomorrow. What stresses others may seem silly to you, and what stresses you may seem like no big deal to others. It has been said, "It's not stress that kills us; it is our reaction to it."[1]

Constant stress keeps our flight-or-fight reactions on constant alert level. Living on the razor edge of either exploding in anger or escaping in fear is a miserable way to live.

- The Fight Reaction: irritable, angry, defensive, argumentative, mad, pouting, critical, tense, complaining, discontent, self-focused, controlling
- The Flight Reaction: fearful, depressed, anxious, discouraged, moody, refusal to communicate, tend to escape by hiding in your work, TV, Internet presence, food, etc.

Knowing that no list is exhaustive, here is a feeble attempt to list six common stressors that seem to reveal their ugly heads when we least expect them.

- **S**in problems
- **T**ime problems
- **R**elationship problems
- **E**nergy problems
- **S**ecurity problems
- **S**piritual maturity problems

To trust more and stress less, we need to be on constant guard for both the common and uncommon stressors of life and combat them with a biblical perspective that comes from the words of Jesus Himself.

Sin Problems

Sin causes stress. Just think about how stressful guilt is. You can only play hide and seek with your sin for so long. Your sin will come to light. Even though conviction is God's merciful way of warning us of the kind of choices and attitudes that only result in more debilitating stress, it is still stressful to sense the convicting hand of God. Sin often brings with it embarrassing consequences. Shame is stressful. Just the thought that others now know how pitiful and weak you really are pushes the stress level higher and higher. Sin often causes tension, and tension is stressful. For proud people even the thought of asking for forgiveness from others (or from God) is a huge stressor.

Simply stated, sin causes stress.

The stress of knowing that there is tension between you and God can be excruciating. Anger, fear, lust, and worry all carry their own levels of stress. Living in the midst of any of these will keep your stress level (and that of others around you) at a fever pitch. The only way to relieve the stress of conviction is to change; the only way to relieve the stress of guilt is to seek forgiveness from God and those involved. Both commands are wrapped with a promise.

What has God said in His Word about sin?

> He that covereth his sins shall not prosper: but whoso confesseth and forsaketh them shall have mercy. (Prov. 28:13)

> If we confess our sins, he is faithful and just to forgive us our sins, and to cleanse us from all unrighteousness. (1 John 1:9)

> Blessed is he whose transgression is forgiven, whose sin is covered. Blessed is the man unto whom the Lord imputeth not iniquity, and in whose spirit there is no guile. When I kept silence, my bones waxed old through my roaring all the day long. For day and night thy hand was heavy upon me: my moisture is turned into the drought of summer. Selah. I acknowledged my sin unto thee, and mine iniquity have I not hid. I said, I will confess my transgressions unto the Lord; and thou forgavest the iniquity of my sin. Selah. (Ps. 32:1–6)

Time Problems

Deadlines cause stress. Time limits hang over your head until the task is completed and the deadline is met. Obviously time limits and deadlines are a necessary part of life, and we would be in an even bigger mess without them, so we would do well to ask ourselves some pointed questions about our stressful and self-imposed deadlines.

- What are the negative consequences of not meeting my deadlines?
- How many other people are affected by my missed deadlines?
- What is the main reason for my not meeting a deadline: not starting early enough or not setting a realistic goal?

The constant battle between punctuality and lateness causes great stress for both the *on-timer* and the *always-later*. The early bird and latecomer stress each other out almost every time they leave the house. Although being on time is not a big deal to some, the early bird has the upper hand on this issue. Those who are habitually late or just on time by the skin of their teeth would be wise to ask themselves these questions.

- How much stress is involved in rushing around and still being late?
- If punctuality is defined as showing high esteem for others and their time, how would you define lateness?
- What are the negative consequences of being on time? What are the positive consequences of being on time?
- Remember that the early bird never goes hungry (if you like worms).

Some are constantly stressed out because they feel they have too little time. There are just not enough hours in a day. By the time you finish your work responsibilities and family obligations, is there any time left for you—or God? Would God ask you to do more than He would be willing to give you time for? Does a weeklong time study reveal any blocks of wasted time?

Would you be willing to put yourself on a time budget? How much time each week do you spend on each of the following?

- Work
- Travel
- Sleeping

- TV
- Online
- Eating
- Exercise
- Getting ready
- Shopping
- Searching because you are too disorganized to find things
- Cleaning, protecting, and working around too much stuff
- Spending time in God's Word and prayer

Have you ever really stopped to think about how short life is, and how little time you really have left in life? If by God's mercy you live to be seventy years old, then you can calculate how much time you have already spent and how much you have left.

- Seventy years is 840 months.
- Seventy years is 3,640 weeks.
- Seventy years is 25,550 days.
- Seventy years is 613,200 hours.
- Seventy years is 36,792,000 minutes.

Do the math. As I write this study, I am sixty years old. I have already used up 21,900 of my 25,550 days.

That is startling! I only have 3,650 days left if God allows me to live until I am seventy.

Maybe this is why God tells us not only to number our days but also to be diligent and wise with the way we invest our time. Take a minute and think about a few of these reminders from God's Word.

> So teach us to number our days, that we may apply our hearts unto wisdom. (Ps. 90:12)

> To everything there is a season, and a time to every purpose under the heaven. (Eccl. 3:1)

> Redeeming the time, because the days are evil. (Eph. 5:16)

> Remember how short my time is: wherefore hast thou made all men in vain? (Ps. 89:47)

> Now my days are swifter than a post: they flee away, they see no good. They are passed away as the swift ships: as the eagle that hasteth to the prey. (Job 9:25–26)

> Man is like to vanity: his days are as a shadow that passeth away. (Ps. 144:4)

> Whereas ye know not what shall be on the morrow. For what is your life? It is even a vapour, that appeareth for a little time, and then vanisheth away. (James 4:14)

Walk in wisdom toward them that are without, re-
deeming the time. (Col. 4:5)

Relationship Problems

No Relationships

- I am lonely and probably always will be.
- There is something wrong with me or I would be married by now.
- Only those who have it together get together.

Bad Relationships

- Am I stuck in this relationship for the rest of my life?
- Maybe my views of divorce are a bit too narrow. I need relief!
- If he or she would just change, everything would be OK.

Questionable Relationships

- Do my friends help me draw closer to God and closer to my family?
- If I changed my lifestyle, would my friends still be my friends?

- How often does the God factor enter our conversations?

What wisdom has God already given regarding relationships?

> I am a companion of all them that fear thee, and of them that keep thy precepts. (Ps. 119:63)

> He that walketh with wise men shall be wise: but a companion of fools shall be destroyed. (Prov. 13:20)

> Therefore if you bring your gift to the altar, and there remember that your brother has something against you, leave your gift there before the altar, and go your way. First be reconciled to your brother, and then come and offer your gift. (Matt. 5:23–24 NKJV)

Energy Problems

Do you lack energy? Are you tired all the time?

- Do you wake up as tired as when you went to bed?
- Do you keep a two-year supply of energy drinks available?
- Do you feel that if you can't go 100 miles an hour (like others) you'll just coast along at 25 mph?

(Have you ever considered bumping your cruise up to 50 mph?)

Do eating habits affect energy problems?

- Are you a junk-food-a-holic? Chip-a-holic? Choc-oholic? (Now, ice cream? Let's pretend that's fine!)
- Do you comfort yourself by eating?
- Do you need to go on a diet? Are you willing to do so?

Does consistent exercise affect energy problems?

- Do you purposefully exercise? Do you *need* to purposefully exercise?
- If you knew you would die in a year if you did not exercise, would it make a difference? Do you have to wait for a doctor's order to start a consistent exercising program?
- If you were promised a better quality of life (more energy, feel younger, greater endurance) what would you be willing to do?

Do sleep habits affect energy problems?

What good advice does God give us from His Word about sleep?

I will both lay me down in peace, and sleep: for
Thou, Lord, only makest me dwell in safety.
(Ps. 4:8)

The sleep of a labouring man is sweet, whether he
eat little or much: but the abundance of the rich will
not suffer him to sleep. (Eccl. 5:12)

But they that wait upon the Lord shall renew their
strength; they shall mount up with wings as eagles;
they shall run, and not be weary; and they shall
walk, and not faint. (Isa. 40:31)

Security Problems

Insecurity is the state of feeling or being subject to danger or injury, the lack of confidence, the lack of secure boundaries, the insecure feeling of rejection, or feeling scared to death! Insecurity comes in various ways.

Financial Security

- What is your standard of living? What is your standard of giving? What is your standard of saving?

- What do you own that brings added stress into your life? Are you willing to throw it away or even give it away?
- Do you have a budget? Have you sought counsel from a godly financial expert?

Eternal Security

- Do you doubt your salvation?
- Do you fear eternity?
- Is your lack of assurance based on a lack of sanctification or spiritual growth?

What do you need God to say to you to make you totally secure? What does an all-powerful, sovereign God say about security?

> But my God shall supply all your need according to his riches in glory by Christ Jesus. (Phil. 4:19)

> In God I will praise his word, in God I have put my trust; I will not fear what flesh can do unto me. (Ps. 56:4)

> The Lord is on my side; I will not fear: what can man do unto me? (Ps. 118:6)

Spiritual Maturity Problems

Signs of Immaturity

- Takes no responsibility for anything, but plays the victim by consistently blame shifting, making excuses, or proving that he or she is a unique exception to the rules (Ps. 52; Prov. 5:22)
- Talks too much and listens too little (James 1:19–20)
- Is easily swayed, easily pressured, and lets acceptance by others be the ultimate decision maker (Eph. 4:13–15)
- Shows insecurity by incessantly trying to impress others by becoming the hero of every story (John 3:30; Col. 1:18)

Signs of Spiritual Immaturity

- Not growing as a Christian in grace, in love, or in understanding
- Falling more than walking, like a spiritual toddler
- Constant falling produces constant stress

The spiritually immature love the first three items listed as the "fruit of the Spirit" (Gal. 5:22)—*love, joy,* and *peace*—but they usually stop there. They may start out their Christian experience wanting to diligently add to their faith (2 Peter 1), but too many leapfrog over the foundational character traits and land on the love and kindness (which are wonderful and needful in our lives), which leads to spiritual immaturity.

Signs of Spiritual Maturity

The spiritually mature are willing to seek the more selfless fruit, such as *patience* toward those who are irritating, *kindness* to the mean-spirited, *goodness* when it is not popular to do so, *faithfulness* when loyalties are tested and dependability is on the line, *gentleness* when harsh words are running through the mind, and *self-control* when the lusts are screaming to be fulfilled.

The spiritually mature pursue the ABCs necessary for true maturity.

- **Virtue** is seen in a man or a woman with strong character and moral excellence.
- **Knowledge** takes dedicated time and the willingness to get up early or stay up late to pour over the Scriptures.
- **Self-control** requires saying no to your supersized appetites and fleshly-born laziness.

- **Perseverance** is a mature, enduring quality that never quits when things get tough. It is the inward strength to withstand stress to accomplish God's best.
- **Godliness** is God-like-ness. Christlikeness is not just "What *would* Jesus do?" but "What *did* Jesus do?" and "What does Jesus continue to do?"
- **Brotherly kindness** shows merciful graciousness to others, even if the recipients are unworthy or acting like jerks.
- **Love** is both a love for God and a love for others that puts the love for self on the back burner.

Meditation!

Let's Think About It.

Meditation is essential for anyone who desires to handle stress God's way. Much of the information in this introduction is a repeat of the first volume of this series entitled *Lest You Fall*. The same principles of meditation apply whether you are wrestling with impurity, anger, bitterness, fear, worry, anxiety, or stress.

The word translated "meditation" throughout Scripture is also translated "imagine" (Ps. 2:1; 38:12), "studieth" (Prov. 15:28; 24:2), "utter," "mutter," "talk," or "speak" (Job 27:4; Ps. 37:30; 71:24; Prov. 8:7); and "mourn" (Isa. 16:7; 38:14; 59:11). It is usually defined as "murmuring," or speaking to oneself. How often do we as believers devote a full morning to studying, imagining, talking through, or speaking to ourselves (meditating) about one specific characteristic of God taught in His Word?

Meditation is a form of creative thinking. Through word studies, comparisons with other passages, and a good study Bible, we can understand what God is saying and how to apply it in a life-changing way. For instance, if we set aside an entire hour to "think about" or meditate on how much God loves righteousness and hates evil, our thinking will be affected in such a way that we will personally begin loving good and hating evil more.

Meditation is essential for a full understanding of God's Word. Most of us have developed lazy habits in reading, grammar, syntax, and word study. We often glance over a word we think we know rather than gaze into its true intent and purpose. For instance, when Paul uses the phrase "for this cause," it is so easy to just keep reading rather than to stop and think, "What cause? What is this driving force in Paul's life? What was his essential reason for living? What is my ultimate reason, purpose, or cause for living? Have I attached myself to a cause bigger than myself, my wants, my time, and my life?" Now Paul's simple phrase "for this cause" takes on a new relevance, and my heart is convicted because I have been living for my own "causes" and not God's.

Meditation is essential for all who seek victory over excessive stress. Paralyzing stress and anxiety come from a lack of knowledge, a misunderstanding of Bible principles, and a misapplication of scriptural truths. We have read many of the passages that deal with the stressors of life but have not thought about them in a way that impacts our hearts. The purpose of this book is to encourage those who desire to free themselves from debilitating stress to meditate on the very words of God that deal with trusting more and stressing less. What God has already given us in His written Word are the very words He would speak to us if we were in a one-on-one counseling situation with Him. As you will see, we will meditate on over one hundred verses from over forty passages that specifically deal with the issues of stress, anxiety, and worry. At the end of this book, hopefully you will be able to take what you have learned and meditate on other passages of Scripture that deal with all kinds of life issues in the same way.

We can live joyful, secure, confident lives free from disabling stress as we begin thinking like God thinks. This takes time. This takes energy. This takes meditation! Now—let's think about it.

Meditate upon these things; give thyself wholly to them; that thy profiting may appear to all. (1 Tim. 4:15)

Meditation Should Delight Us!

I will meditate in thy precepts, and have respect unto thy ways. I will delight myself in thy statutes: I will not forget thy word. (Ps. 119:15–16)

Blessed is the man that walketh not in the counsel of the ungodly, nor standeth in the way of sinners, nor sitteth in the seat of the scornful. But his delight is in the law of the Lord; and in his law doth he meditate day and night. (Ps. 1:1–2)

My meditation of him shall be sweet: I will be glad in the Lord. (Ps. 104:34)

Meditation Should Consume Us!

Let the words of my mouth, and the meditation of my heart, be acceptable in thy sight, O Lord, my strength, and my redeemer. (Ps. 19:14)

O how love I thy law! It is my meditation all the day. (Ps. 119:97)

Mine eyes prevent the night watches, that I might meditate in thy word. (Ps. 119:148)

Meditation Should Control Us!

This book of the law shall not depart out of thy mouth; but thou shalt meditate therein day and night, that thou mayest observe to do according to all that is written therein: for then thou shalt make thy way prosperous, and then thou shalt have good success. (Josh. 1:8)

The Mechanics of Meditation

"How do you do this?"

In some areas of life, there is danger in being a do-it-yourselfer. I know enough about working on cars to get a job started but often not enough to finish it. Some do-it-yourself plumbers, with the goal of simply replacing a faucet, can turn their bathroom into a water park complete with fountains and pools. But there are other times when it is essential to be a do-it-yourselfer. Meditation is one of those times. It is something that we must learn to do ourselves. We can read books, listen to messages, and allow others to meditate for us, or we can study, labor, and master the art of exegesis (careful explanation or interpretation of a biblical text) in order to enjoy meaningful meditation for ourselves. This is definitely a do-it-yourself discipline of the Christian life.

Anyone can meditate. Everyone should meditate. But most don't even try. If you were not interested in lessening your stress by trusting God more, you probably would not even be reading this book. What you need is a meditation toolbox that is filled with the proper meditation tools. I would encourage you to get one tool at a time and practice using it until you have mastered it. Don't fall into the trap of filling up your toolbox with specialty tools that you never use.

Tool 1: Your Bible

Read . . . read . . . READ! Read the passage you are studying over and over again. Sometimes comparing various translations as commentaries helps with your understanding of what you are reading.

Tool 2: A Study Bible

Study Bibles are a tremendous help in understanding the intent and purpose of any given passage. Sometimes a simple clarification of the audience, customs, geographical considerations, or unusual word usages can help you to understand what God was saying to those people at that time. Bible scholars, trained in hermeneutics and Bible interpretation, have given their lives to help many Bible readers fully understand why God wrote what He wrote in His Word.

Tool 3: Word-Study Helps

There are many words in our English Bible whose meanings have changed over the years and have almost become obsolete in conversation today. Words like *concupiscence, superfluity, wantonness, lasciviousness, lucre, guile,* and *quickened* are not found in most of the letters, e-mails, or text messages we read on a daily basis. Word-study helps such as *Strong's Concordance, Vine's Expository Dictionary,* Zodhiates's *Complete Word Study Dictionary,* Robertson's *New Testament Word Pictures,* Vincent's *New Testament Word Studies, Theological Wordbook of the Old Testament,* and Greek and Hebrew lexicons open up the meanings to words we commonly glance over as we read. Words are powerful. Because we often do not know the true meanings of certain words, we miss their intent and cannot personally apply the passage as we should.

Tool 4: Bible Dictionaries and Encyclopedias

Most of us have not grown up in the Holy Land, lived in Egypt, or sailed the Mediterranean. I personally have never fished with a net, hunted with a bow, or plowed with an ox. A good Bible dictionary or encyclopedia can help you feel the heat of the desert and understand the difficulty of sailing through a stormy sea. I would suggest *International Standard Bible Encyclopedia*, *Zondervan's Pictorial Bible Dictionary*, *Nelson's New Illustrated Bible Dictionary*, or *Unger's Bible Dictionary* to start with.

Tool 5: Commitment of Time

All the tools available are to no avail without a commitment of time and a commitment to concentration. Meditation takes time. We seem to have the time to do what we *want* but not the time to do what we *should*. Consistency in spending extended periods of time in God's Word is a key to proper meditation. Any time is a good time, but if you give God, say, one-half hour every morning before you get pulled into your fast and furious daily routine, you will actually wake up in the morning looking forward to spending that time with God. (By the way, if you think you are too busy, consider that this kind of meditation in God's Word will simply replace the wasted time it takes to sin.)

Tool 6: A Set Place

Finding the right place to ensure complete concentration is also a must. Unless you have a set place to meditate, distractions can easily cause your mind to drift. Find a place where you are isolated, or at least insulated, from the distractions of TV, newspapers, radio, children, friends, and weariness. Find a place where it is just you and God, and it is almost like the whole world disappears for those few minutes each morning.

Tool 7: Prayer

Talk to God. Ask God to open your eyes and your heart to what He is saying. Ask God for wisdom; He promises to give it to you. Ask God for understanding; He wants you to understand. Ask God for insight into His heart. Ask God to help you think as He thinks, to look at sin as He looks at sin, to love kindness and forgiveness as He loves kindness and forgiveness. Your goal is to defeat the anger in your heart by having the mind of Christ. When your meditation becomes your mindset, you will be amazed at your understanding of Scripture and your progress in consistent victory over selfish, sinful thinking. You'll also be pleasing God and not self.

Before we step into the heart of this book, let's walk through one short passage—Matthew 5:5—using the tools mentioned above. What words do we need to study and understand so we do not miss their meaning and intent? What word pictures do these words bring to mind that will help us not only fully understand what they are saying, but also apply in such a way that they evoke a stronger love for God and a more intense hatred for sin? What is God saying to us?

This is what God says.

Matthew 5:5

Blessed are the meek: for they shall inherit the earth.

How can this affect me?

There is a secret strength to meekness. Jesus was meek. The meek keep their strength under control. It is their resolved inner strength that keeps them from totally stressing out.

Why does God choose to bless the meek with such a great inheritance?

Meekness is not weakness, but strength under control. A wild stallion broken and bridled has the same strength it had while it ran wild; the difference is that the strength is now controlled by its rider. Who is in control of your life? On a scale of one to ten, how are you doing on your meekness chart? Who controls your devotional life? You or God? Who controls your thought life? You or God? Who controls your emotions? You or God? Who controls you? You or God?

Meekness keeps you cool when everyone around you is getting heated up. Meekness keeps you settled when others are exploding with rage. Meekness is an attitude of the heart that always puts God and others first.

How do you respond when your family or friends are unreasonable, irrational, or simply don't even try to understand your viewpoint, your wants, or your needs?

Those who view meekness as gutless, weak, or spineless are shocked and sometimes even embarrassed when they realize the inner boldness, strength, and confidence of a truly meek person.

You can often tell a lot about a person by the friends that they choose. Meekness is seldom seen alone in Scripture but is surrounded with some wonderful friends. You've probably met some of them—Humility, Patience, Kindness, Gentleness, Self-control, Approachability, and Genuine Sincerity.

Which of your closest friends or family members could be identified by one or more of these eight characteristics of meekness? (By the way, you can find these friends listed in passages like Galatians 5:22–23, Ephesians 4:2, Colossians 3:12, 1 Timothy 6:11, and James 3:17.)

"Ladies and gentlemen!" A godly lady has a meek and quiet spirit. A godly gentleman is a meek man. Meekness pleases God. A meek person keeps the powerful desires of lust and the intense passions of anger under control. The strength of a meek person is seen in his refusal to be controlled by all the intense desires of his weak flesh.

Jesus was meek! He created the world yet allowed it to crucify Him. He is God, yet He permitted mere men to spit on Him. He humbly submitted to His Father's plan. Read Matthew 11:28–30. Just as a young bull learns from the older bull by being yoked together to pull a plow or a wagon, we can learn from yoking ourselves up closely to our Lord Jesus. In what specific ways has Jesus modeled for us a meek and lowly example?

The proud, haughty, and discontented will not inherit the earth—no matter how much they desire it or think they deserve it. It is the meek and the humble that will inherit the earth. *Blessed are the meek.*

The meek shall eat and be satisfied. (Ps. 22:26)

The Lord lifts up the humble [meek]. (Ps. 147:6 NKJV)

The meek also shall increase their joy in the Lord. (Isa. 29:19)

The meek shall inherit the earth; and shall delight themselves in the abundance of peace. (Ps. 37:11)

Part *One*

What Does Christ Want Us to *Know* to Stress Less and Trust More?

Meditation 1

Stressed or blessed?

This is what God says.

Matthew 5:3–10

Blessed are the poor in spirit: for theirs is the kingdom of heaven.

Blessed are they that mourn: for they shall be comforted.

Blessed are the meek: for they shall inherit the earth.

Blessed are they which do hunger and thirst after righteousness: for they shall be filled.

Blessed are the merciful: for they shall obtain mercy.

Blessed are the pure in heart: for they shall see God.

Blessed are the peacemakers: for they shall be called the children of God.

Blessed are they which are persecuted for righteousness' sake: for theirs is the kingdom of heaven.

How can this affect me?

Those who are controlled by stress don't often use the phrase, "Happily ever after!" Without Christ, true happiness is only a fairy tale. There are no magic wands that mystically and magically produce biblical happiness.

Would you rather be blessed or stressed? It is not just a coincidence that Christ uses the comforting words "blessed are" nine times in the first part of His Sermon on the Mount. What does it mean to be blessed? Whether you say it with one syllable or two, it is a wonderful word, a wonderful principle, and a wonderful feeling—to be blessed, to feel blessed, to know that someone loves you enough to bless you. True biblical blessing from God is much more than a southern "bless your heart" greeting or a kind "bless you" when you sneeze.

So the answer to the question "What does it mean to be blessed?" is found in words like *redemption*, *salvation*, and *reconciliation*. God's wonderful redemptive plan is the purest picture of true blessing that can be portrayed. Such blessing is complete with seven promises to those who have personally received God's gift of salvation by faith in Christ.

Jesus answered these seven questions in the introduction of His message in Matthew 5:3–10.

- Who will be part of the kingdom of heaven?
- Who will be comforted?
- Who will inherit the earth?
- Who will be filled with the righteousness of Christ?
- Who will obtain mercy?
- Who will see God?
- Who will be called the children of God?

Look closely. This list is interestingly and intricately tied together in a logical progression. Those who see and acknowledge their pitiful, spiritual poverty will mourn because of it. They will relinquish control of their lives to God, begin hungering and thirsting for God's righteousness, progressively become like their Lord as they grow in mercy and purity, be used by God to reconcile men to Him and each other, and be rejected and persecuted by those who recognize them as the children of almighty God.

Nothing could be more stressful than the realization that I am fully responsible to pay the penalty for my selfishness and sin—which, according to Romans 6:23, is eternal death. God came to earth in the bodily form of Jesus Christ. Jesus never sinned! Therefore, when He was crucified, He did not die to pay for His own sins, but for the sins of all who will trust in His sacrificial death for them. He was born to die for you and me!

Jesus provided the way for us all to be reconciled to God forever. And therefore, we are blessed. Blessed by God with eternal, everlasting life.

Meditation 2

Truly blessed are the poor in spirit.

This is what God says.

Matthew 5:3

Blessed are the poor in spirit: for theirs is the kingdom of heaven.

How can this affect me?

Does the thought of eternity stress you out? Jesus begins His message by answering the simple question, "What does a true child of God look like?" Who would know how to describe the heart of a true believer better than Jesus Himself? Don't be anxious. Don't be stressed. Salvation is for all. The conditions necessary for entering into God's kingdom are a vital part of the character of those who live in God's kingdom. Why is being "poor in spirit" essential for God's blessing? Those who are poor in spirit admit their own spiritual poverty.

You know you are poor in spirit when you see your emptiness, helplessness, and deservedness of all the judgment your sinfulness has accumulated. Those who are blinded to their own worthlessness are proud and do not understand this kind of brokenness before God. Never forget Paul's reminder in Ephesians 2:8–9, "For by grace are ye saved through faith; and that not of yourselves: it is the gift of God: Not of works, lest any man should boast."

What is Christ's promise to those who admit their spiritual need? "The kingdom of heaven!" Think about it. Wouldn't you rather have the kingdom of heaven than any kingdom that exists here on earth? A great way to relieve stress is to thank God for His willingness to offer us the undeserved privilege of being a part of His eternal kingdom. Those who are poor in spirit are truly rich in God's grace.

> To this man will I look, even to him that is poor [humble] and of a contrite spirit, and trembleth at my word. (Isa. 66:2)

Meditation 3

Genuinely blessed are those who mourn.

This is what God says.

Matthew 5:4

Blessed are they that mourn: for they shall be comforted.

How can this affect me?

Sad. Glad. Sorrowful. Happy. Troubled. Comforted. Stressed. Unstressed. Unless we understand the context and intent of Matthew 5:4, it really does not make much sense. How can we be happy and sad at the same time?

"Happy are they that are sad." This statement contradicts itself unless you see the cause for such sadness and the comfort that God promises through His forgiveness.

For godly sorrow worketh repentance to salvation not to be repented of: but the sorrow of the world worketh death. (2 Cor. 7:10)

When was the last time you cried? I mean really cried when you realized that your sin grieves God and hurts others? Once you are overwhelmed with your own spiritual poverty and understand the gravity of your own depravity, you will *mourn*. You will feel like weeping because of your sin. When godly sorrow truly grips a heart, tears often flow. Although this may seem stressful, it is not a hopeless stress. Can you remember the moment you realized you were a sinner in need of forgiveness? Do you remember how that sense of guilt broke your heart knowing that you had sinned against a loving God? Can you remember how that felt?

Conviction saddens a heart. Forgiveness gladdens a heart.

"They shall be comforted." Now here is a promise that can replace our tears with a smile and our "stressed-ness" with a blessedness. I grieve that my own sin sent my Lord to the cross. The guilt and disappointment over my own selfishness are overwhelming. Now our Lord reminds us that for those who mourn over their sinfulness, forgiveness is not only available, but offered freely by the very One we have sinned against. This is so comforting!

If you want to smile your way through tearful eyes, quote 1 John 1:8–9, and then thank God for what these precious verses teach. Those who refuse to admit their sinful condition and mourn over their wickedness will never experience the joy and happiness of God's undeserved forgiveness. When we admit we are sinners, then we can smile. When we confess our sins to our Lord, then the stress of guilt and conviction disappears.

> If we say that we have no sin, we deceive ourselves, and the truth is not in us. If we confess our sins, he [God] is faithful and just to forgive us our sins, and to cleanse us from all unrighteousness. (1 John 1:8–9)

David wept until he could weep no more because of his unconfessed sin and broken relationship with God (Ps. 32:4). Peter wept bitterly, moved by sorrow over his sin (Luke 22:62). Jesus wept. Not because of His own sin, but because of the sin of those He loved who had rejected Him. "[Jesus] beheld the city, and wept over it." (Luke 19:41). We should weep when we understand what Paul, Isaiah, and Peter wrote.

> As it is written, There is none righteous, no, not one: there is none that understandeth, there is none that seeketh after God. They are all gone out of the way, they are together become unprofitable; there is none that doeth good, no, not one. (Rom. 3:10–12)

> All we like sheep have gone astray; we have turned every one to his own way; and the Lord hath laid on Him the iniquity of us all. (Isa. 53:6)

> For Christ also hath once suffered for sins, the just for the unjust, that He might bring us to God, being put to death in the flesh, but quickened by the Spirit. (1 Peter 3:18)

We can rejoice when we understand David's, Solomon's, and Paul's words.

> Blessed is he whose transgression is forgiven, whose sin is covered. Blessed is the man unto whom the Lord imputeth not iniquity, and in whose spirit there is no guile. When I kept silence, my bones waxed old through my roaring all the day long. For day and night thy hand was heavy upon me: my moisture is turned into the drought of summer. Selah. I acknowledged my sin unto thee, and mine iniquity have I not hid. I said, I will confess my transgressions unto the Lord; and thou forgavest the iniquity of my sin. Selah. (Ps. 32:1–5)

There is therefore now no condemnation to them which are in Christ Jesus, who walk not after the flesh, but after the Spirit. (Rom. 8:1)

For whosoever shall call upon the name of the Lord shall be saved. (Rom. 10:13)

He that covereth his sins shall not prosper: but whoso confesseth and forsaketh them shall have mercy. (Prov. 28:13)

Meditation 4

Exceptionally blessed are the meek.

This is what God says.

Matthew 5:5

Blessed are the meek: for they shall inherit the earth.

How can this affect me?

There is a secret strength to meekness. Jesus was meek. The meek keep their strength under control. It is their resolved inner strength that keeps them from totally stressing out.

Why does God choose to bless the meek with such a great inheritance?

Meekness is not weakness but strength under control. A wild stallion broken and bridled has the same strength it had while it ran wild; the difference is that the strength is now controlled by its rider. Who is in control of your life? On a scale of one to ten, how are you doing on your meekness chart? Who controls your devotional life? You or God? Who controls your thought life? You or God? Who controls your emotions? You or God? Who controls you? You or God?

Meekness opposes not only pride, it opposes stubbornness, pigheadedness, and a vengeful heart that seeks retaliation instead of reconciliation. Commentator Arthur Pink says, "Meekness is the opposite of *self-will* toward God and *ill-will* toward men."[1]

Meekness keeps you cool when everyone around you is getting heated up.

Meekness keeps you settled when others are exploding with rage.

Meekness is an attitude of the heart that always puts God and others first.

How do you respond when your family or friends are unreasonable, irrational, or simply don't even try to understand your viewpoint, your wants, or your needs?

Those who view meekness as gutless, weak, or spineless are shocked and sometimes even embarrassed when they realize the inner boldness, strength, and confidence of a truly meek person.

You can often tell a lot about a person by the friends that they choose. Meekness is seldom seen alone in Scripture but surrounds itself with some wonderful friends. You've probably met some of them: Humility, Patience, Kindness, Gentleness, Self-control, Approachability, and Genuine Sincerity.

Which of your closest friends or family members could be identified by one or more of these eight characteristics of meekness? (By the way, you can find these friends listed in passages like Galatians 5:22–23, Ephesians 4:2, Colossians 3:12, 1 Timothy 6:11, and James 3:17.)

"Ladies and gentlemen!" A godly lady has a meek and quiet spirit. A godly gentleman is a meek man. Meekness pleases God. A meek person keeps the powerful desires of lust and the intense passions of anger under control. The strength of a meek person is seen in his or her refusal to be controlled by all the intense desires of the person's weak flesh.

Jesus was meek. He created the world yet allowed it to crucify Him. He is God, yet He permitted mere men to spit on Him. He humbly submitted to His Father's plan. Read Matthew 11:28–30. Just as a young bull learns from the older bull by being yoked together to pull a plow or a wagon, we can learn from being yoked closely to our Lord Jesus. In what specific ways has Jesus modeled for us a meek and lowly example?

The proud, haughty, and discontented will not inherit the earth, no matter how much they desire it or think they deserve it. It is the meek and the humble that will inherit the earth. "Blessed are the meek."

The meek shall eat and be satisfied. (Ps. 22:26)

The Lord lifteth up the meek. (Ps. 147:6)

The meek also shall increase their joy in the Lord. (Isaiah 29:19)

The meek shall inherit the earth; and shall delight themselves in the abundance of peace. (Ps. 37:11)

Meditation 5

Greatly blessed are they who hunger
and thirst after righteousness.

This is what God says.

Matthew 5:6

Blessed are they which do hunger and thirst after
righteousness: for they shall be filled.

How can this affect me?

Have you ever been really hungry? Now I don't
mean that you were on the brink of starvation because
Thanksgiving dinner was pushed from 12:00 noon to
1:00. I mean so starved that you could not think of anything but food. Most of us in some way are into food. A
half hour on the *Food Network* watching shows hosted
from all around the world featuring bizarre, overindul-
gent, appetizing foods may make us hungry, but not

starving. How many times a day or a week do you think about food or about something to drink? Our Lord is using a great illustration here to help us recognize how desperate we should be for the only kind of righteousness that satisfies a holy God. Think back to when you were so convicted over your own sinfulness that you cried out to God and pled to be forgiven and cleansed. Do you remember that intense desire to be saved from your sin, forgiven of your sin, and cleansed from your sin so that you could finally be in a right relationship with God?

> For I say unto you, That except your righteousness
> shall exceed the righteousness of the scribes and
> Pharisees, ye shall in no case enter into the king-
> dom of heaven. (Matt. 5:20)

Trying to be good, or I should say, *good enough,* is stressful. There is no end to it! Even if we seem to be doing good for a couple weeks or even a month, then we mess up, do something stupid, selfish, or sinful, and fall. Stress eats us up as we strive to reach this unattainable goal. The righteousness that satisfies a holy God cannot be earned or personally attained. It is a free gift from God to all who admit their helplessness and choose to trust Christ's sacrificial work on the cross. Christ died for us so that we can live with God.

Our spiritual appetites reveal our spiritual attitudes. If we hunger and thirst after our own righteousness, we will always remain hungry and thirsty (and stressed). If we hunger and thirst after Christ's righteousness, we will be filled. It is interesting that our Lord Jesus did not ask what we enjoy snacking on or nibbling at. Think about it. There is no desperation in desiring a Snickers bar or a Pop-Tart. God designed hunger and thirst to keep us hydrated and nutritionally satisfied. Spiritual hunger and spiritual thirst work the same way. So are you hungry? Thirsty? Passionately desirous to be right with God?

The Pharisees portrayed an external righteousness that was viewed by most as unattainable. Even if people wanted to be *that good* and *that righteous*, they kept messing up and breaking all the legalistic rules of the Pharisees. What most do not understand is that even the righteousness of the scribes and Pharisees falls short of the righteousness needed to enter heaven. God's level of righteousness is perfection! Trying to be perfect is stressful. Actually perfection is impossible to achieve no matter how sincere, how nice, how good, or how self-righteous you are. How many times do we need to sin to be a sinner? Once! Romans 3:23 reminds us about our inability to attain or reach God's glorious perfection in our own power.

If you passionately attempt to be good enough to work your way into heaven, you will live under constant stress. Working your way to heaven is not going to happen. The only righteousness that is acceptable to God's standard is what Christ fulfilled while He lived a perfect life on earth. God is willing to give (*impute* is the fancy word) that righteousness to us if we simply believe in His precious gospel message: Jesus lived for us; Jesus died for us; Jesus rose from the dead for us. Meditate on these three verses and tell the Lord, "Thank You, thank You, thank You" for what He has done for us. Don't stress. Just trust.

> For he hath made him [Jesus] to be sin for us, who knew no sin; that we might be made the righteousness of God in him. (2 Cor. 5:21)

> Not by works of righteousness which we have done, but according to his mercy he saved us, by the washing of regeneration, and renewing of the Holy Ghost. (Titus 3:5)

Abraham believed God, and it was accounted to him for righteousness. (Gal. 3:6)

Meditation 6

Extremely blessed are the merciful.

This is what God says.

Matthew 5:7

Blessed are the merciful: for they shall obtain mercy.

How can this affect me?

Why is it important for us to be as merciful to others as God has been to us?

A close self-examination will cause most of us to cry "Mercy!" Not only do we know how selfish and wicked our thoughts are, we know that God knows too. What if God refused to forgive us and punished us according to what is deep down in our hearts and minds? How stressful would it be for you to know that when you stand before God, He would unleash His wrath on you for everything that you have thought or done?

Sadly too many treat others who have sinned against them the exact opposite of how they want to be treated by God.

The attitude of those who live in God's kingdom is not self-serving, harsh, cruel, or calloused. It is merciful—full of mercy. It hurts with those who hurt. It grieves with those who grieve. It cares. It gives to the undeserving without any thought of getting repaid. It is kind to the unkind, helpful to the hateful, and loving to the unloving.

Mercy is an attitude of the soul, which moved by pity is willing to get its hands dirty by helping others who are in trouble. It is more than just caring. It actually does something to help. God often allows and even orchestrates difficulties that prepare us to be able to comfort someone else who will face the same trial in the future. Just to know that our trials are not a waste but actually enable us to comfort others gives purpose to hardships we face in life. Remember, the God of all comfort comforts us so we can comfort others with the same comfort we were comforted with by our comforting God. 2 Corinthians 1:3–4 states it a bit better.

Blessed be God, even the Father of our Lord Jesus

Christ, the Father of mercies, and the God of all
comfort; who comforteth us in all our tribulation,
that we may be able to comfort them which are in
any trouble, by the comfort wherewith we ourselves
are comforted of God.

Mercy was not common in Galilee during the life of
Christ. Unlike Jesus, who was a perfect model of mercy,
most religious leaders self-righteously looked down on
all who were not just like them. Jesus was merciful to
those whom others would throw away. He picked up
children and touched lepers. He reached out to prosti-
tutes, greedy tax collectors, arrogant religious leaders,
and unbelievers. He offered forgiveness to those who
crucified Him. Jesus was merciful. Jesus is merciful!

Now all of us have to deal with prickly people from
time to time. Prickly people are stressful! They could
be friends, family, coworkers, roommates . . . or even a
spouse. Is there anyone on earth you refuse to forgive?
Can you think of anyone that you look down on or despise? Is there anyone in your life that you refuse to be
merciful to? God promises mercy to the merciful. What
do you think is God's promise to the unmerciful?

But God, who is rich in mercy, for His great love
wherewith He loved us, even when we were dead

in sins, hath quickened us together with Christ, (by grace ye are saved;) and hath raised us up together, and made us sit together in heavenly places in Christ Jesus: that in the ages to come He might shew the exceeding riches of His grace in His kindness toward us through Christ Jesus. (Eph. 2:4–7)

The Lord is merciful and gracious, slow to anger, and plenteous in mercy. (Ps. 103:8)

It is of the Lord's mercies that we are not consumed, because His compassions fail not. They are new every morning: great is Thy faithfulness. (Lam. 3:22–23)

Blessed are the merciful. Pray and ask God to reveal to you how you can become more merciful toward others (even the prickly people) in your life. If you strive to be as merciful to others as God has been to you, you will not only reduce the stress in your life, but also the stress in the lives of those you show mercy.

Meditation 7

Tremendously blessed are the pure in heart.

This is what God says.

Matthew 5:8

Blessed are the pure in heart: for they shall see God.

How can this affect me?

Do you believe that there is a living God?

How stressful would it be to know that you would be separated from God, from heaven, and from everything that is good and godly for all eternity?

Pure hearts see God! This is a promise to claim and an attainable goal to pursue. So if we really want to see God more clearly, we need to understand what the Lord means when He says, "Blessed are the pure in heart, for they shall see God."

Something that is truly *pure* is clean, unsoiled, and free from all pollution and uncleanness.

The "pure in heart" are those whose minds have no hypocrisy or evil intent toward others and whose hearts are clean before God with no hidden, secret, or unconfessed sin.

Your heart is your mind; your mind is your heart. In describing the wickedness of men's hearts prior to Noah's flood, God said, "every imagination of the thoughts of his heart was only evil continually" (Gen. 6:5). Solomon reminds us that a man thinks "in his heart" (Prov. 23:7). Jesus knew the Pharisee's hearts and not only asked them why they thought evil in their hearts but also reminded them their hearts were full of evil thoughts (Matthew 9:4; 15:19).

Does it concern you that the Lord not only can read your thoughts, but actually knows your heart better than you do?

"Blessed are the pure in heart." Happy, truly happy, is the one who can live life out in the open with nothing to hide and absolutely no fear of secret sins being revealed. Purity blossoms into a sweet assurance that you are right with God. It is a joy to live an unhypocritical, sincere, genuinely simplistic life. This of course makes us ask ourselves some real life questions.

- Am I living free from hypocrisy?
- Do I serve God with pure motives?
- Do I really have good intentions toward others?
- Am I phony or insincere in my walk with God?
- Do I keep my mind pure from evil thinking?

> Seeing ye have purified your souls in obeying the truth through the Spirit unto unfeigned love of the brethren, see that ye love one another with a pure heart fervently. (1 Peter 1:22)

> Now the end of the commandment is charity [love] out of a pure heart, and of a good conscience, and of faith unfeigned. (1 Tim. 1:5)

A pure heart runs away from sinful desires as it races toward godliness. By the way, we are reminded that a pure heart always runs better with like-minded, praying friends running by its side.

> Flee also youthful lusts: but follow righteousness, faith, charity, peace, with them that call on the Lord out of a pure heart. (2 Tim. 2:22)

"For they shall see God." Those who live with an inward purity before God and an unmixed sincerity before men have a heart that can see God's power, God's love, and God's presence in a more real way. The excellencies of God's character can be seen clearly from a pure heart, which is part of the kingdom character that God produces in the heart of a true believer.

Think through the progression of the beatitudes found in Matthew 5:3–11. The poor in spirit recognize their spiritual poverty and mourn, crying out to God for His cleansing. The comforting forgiveness from God produces meekness, which stirs the hearts of the poor in spirit to relinquish to God total control of their lives. A true hunger and a passion for God's righteousness begins to grip their heart. They slowly grow in godliness and, like God, become merciful toward others. Their sincere, genuine, pure hearts are seen from the inside out. This is not an act. This is not pretend. These believers are for real.

"For they shall see God." Living in the light of eternity is part of the earthly purity process. Jesus is pure. Someday we will stand in His presence—face to face—with a purity that comes only from Him. Such a wonderful promise should motivate purity in our own hearts until we have been rescued from this impure world. Then we will be able to personally thank God for the purity that comes only from Him—without which no one will ever see God.

> Beloved, now are we the sons of God, and it doth not yet appear what we shall be: but we know that, when he shall appear, we shall be like him; for we shall see him as he is. And every man that hath this hope in him purifieth himself, even as He is pure. (1 John 3:2–3)

A perverse heart is well acquainted with stress. A pure heart keeps stress at a distance.

Meditation 8

Exceedingly blessed are the peacemakers.

This is what God says.

Matthew 5:9

Blessed are the peacemakers: for they shall be called the children of God.

How can this affect me?

Once you experience the peace of God in your own heart, you will want to share it with others.

Peace I leave with you, my peace I give unto you: not as the world giveth, give I unto you. Let not your heart be troubled, neither let it be afraid. (John 14:27)

The peace of God, which passeth all understanding, shall keep your hearts and minds through Christ Jesus. (Phil. 4:7)

How would you define a peacemaker? A peace-faker? A peace-breaker? We have all played these roles. The peace-faker stresses out himself. The peace-breaker stresses out others. Only the peacemaker can be a stress breaker while experiencing peace in his own life and encouraging it in the hearts of others. God gives a true peacemaker three job responsibilities to fulfill.

One: Make peace with God and yourself. This is salvation.

Isn't it wonderful to know that you can be at peace with God? Isn't it a joy to realize that your sin has been dealt with and you have the precious privilege of having a right relationship with God? Isn't living with a calm cheerfulness of soul a wonderful way to live? Take another sip of your coffee and think about how salvation impacts your peace with God.

> Therefore being justified by faith, we have peace with God through our Lord Jesus Christ. (Rom 5:1)

> For it pleased the Father that in Him [Jesus] should all fulness dwell; and, having made peace through the blood of his cross, by him to reconcile all things unto himself; by him, I say, whether they be things in earth, or things in heaven. And you, that were sometime alienated and enemies in your mind by

wicked works, yet now hath he reconciled. (Col. 1:19–21)

Blessed is he whose transgression is forgiven, whose sin is covered. (Ps. 32:1)

But now in Christ Jesus ye who sometimes were far off are made nigh by the blood of Christ. For he is our peace, who hath made both one, and hath broken down the middle wall of partition between us; having abolished in his flesh the enmity, even the law of commandments contained in ordinances; for to make in himself of twain one new man, so making peace; and that he might reconcile both unto God in one body by the cross, having slain the enmity thereby: and came and preached peace to you which were afar off, and to them that were nigh. (Eph. 2:13–17)

Two: Help other people make peace with God. This is evangelism.

Have you ever experienced the joy of leading someone to trust in Christ for their eternal salvation? Have you ever invited someone to church or to hear a gospel message and they chose to put their faith in Christ that very night? Talk about happy! Joyful! Blessed! Joyful are the peacemakers who are used by God to see others become children of God!

We are ambassadors from another world sharing the truth of our eternal world with those who didn't even realize that such a world exists.

> Now then we are ambassadors for Christ, as though God did beseech you by us: we pray you in Christ's stead, be ye reconciled to God. For He [God] hath made Him [Jesus] to be sin for us, who knew no sin; that we might be made the righteousness of God in him. (2 Cor. 5:20–21).

Three: Make peace with other people, and help other people be at peace with each other. This is reconciliation.

If we are not right with others, we are not right with God. (This includes parents, siblings, kids, and friends). We are commanded to do all we can to "live peaceably with all men" (Rom. 12:18). Jesus reminds us to not even worship until we are right with those whom we have offended or with those who in some way have offended us (Matt. 5:23–24). Is there anyone on this earth whom you refuse to forgive? Is there anyone you need to call or go visit in order to be reconciled?

"For they shall be called the children of God." Peacemakers are noticed. Jesus did not say we would be *made* a son of God, but *called* a son of God. When people see your meekness, hunger and thirst for God, mercy, purity, and your willingness to make peace, you will be known as a true Christian. You will be called a child of God. I pray that is so with you. The more you bless others, the less stress will control your life.

> Finally, brethren, farewell. Be perfect, be of good comfort, be of one mind, live in peace; and the God of love and peace shall be with you. (2 Cor. 13:11)

Meditation 9

Especially blessed are the persecuted.

This is what God says.

Matthew 5:10–12

Blessed are they which are persecuted for right-eousness' sake: for theirs is the kingdom of heaven. Blessed are ye, when men shall revile you, and persecute you, and shall say all manner of evil against you falsely, for my sake. Rejoice, and be exceeding glad: for great is your reward in heaven: for so persecuted they the prophets which were before you.

How can this affect me?

Being hated is stressful. Being persecuted is beyond stress. Why do godly, righteous believers become targets for persecution? Why do Christlike believers have to deal with the constant stress of being hated, ridiculed, and misunderstood? How can we be happy and hated at the same time?

Remember what we have learned so far. Once you have seen the reality of your wicked heart, mourned and repented over your sin, surrendered control to God, grown in your spiritual appetites, lived a godly life marked by mercy and purity, and attempted to help others be at peace with God, you will be noticed.

- You will be noticed by heaven and blessed.
- You will be noticed by people and called a child of God.
- You will be noticed by hell, and the persecution will begin.

This is confusing. What God blesses and many people respect, the rest of the world hates. Have you ever been made fun of, laughed at, or looked down on just because you were a Christian? Was it because you tried to witness? Was it because you refused to give in to peer pressure?

When you take a stand for God's name, for God's Word, or for God's honor, someone will get upset. When you accept the Bible as your final authority—even when it defies current culture—a big bull's-eye appears on your back and the stress begins.

When you really think about this, it is absurd. Illogical. Senseless! Why would anyone be upset with those who do right? Wouldn't it make more sense to hate sin, abuse, cruelty, and arrogance? Honestly I don't think it is doing good that upsets unbelievers, but being godly. It is not being kind that is hated, it is living godly in Christ Jesus that is a problem to them.

A life of godliness reproves ungodliness and provokes the ungodly to anger. Those living with a biblical attitude are hated by those who refuse to admit that the Bible is the final authority. They know that if the Bible is right, they are wrong and will stand before God and be accountable for their sin. This clash between "I am in control" and "God is in control" is inevitable.

Instead of being stressed out, how can we "rejoice" when we are mocked, laughed at, or excluded? What are the "rewards" or the advantages of being reproached for the sake of Christ? Peter explains. He reminds us why it is a privilege and an honor to be reproached and hated for Christ's sake.

> Beloved, think it not strange concerning the fiery trial which is to try you, as though some strange

thing happened unto you: but rejoice, inasmuch as ye are partakers of Christ's sufferings; that, when his glory shall be revealed, ye may be glad also with exceeding joy. If ye be reproached for the name of Christ, happy are ye; for the spirit of glory and of God resteth upon you: on their part he is evil spoken of, but on your part he is glorified. But let none of you suffer as a murderer, or as a thief, or as an evildoer, or as a busybody in other men's matters. Yet if any man suffer as a Christian, let him not be ashamed; but let him glorify God on this behalf. (1 Peter 4:12–16)

But and if ye suffer for righteousness' sake, happy are ye: and be not afraid of their terror, neither be troubled. (1 Peter 3:14)

What will the persecution look like in everyday life?

"Blessed are ye, when men shall revile you . . . for my sake." You will be reviled. Verbal abuse has been around since before the time of Christ. Revilers are those who hurl insults and viciously attack with hurtful, abusive words. Words *do* hurt. Matthew reminds us that Jesus was reviled, even as He hung on the cross dying for our sins.

And they that passed by reviled him, wagging their heads. (Matt. 27:39)

Peter tells us how Jesus responded to the angry, abusive shouting.

> For even hereunto were ye called: because Christ also suffered for us, leaving us an example, that ye should follow his steps: Who did no sin, neither was guile found in his mouth: Who, when he was reviled, reviled not again; when he suffered, he threatened not; but committed himself to him that judgeth righteously. (1 Peter 2:21–23)

"Blessed are ye, when men shall persecute you . . . for my sake." You will be persecuted. Although biblical persecution and modern-day peer pressure differ in severity, they have a similar purpose. Persecution uses both verbal and physical threats to pressure believers into turning their backs on Jesus Christ. What did persecution look like when Stephen, James, and later Paul shared Christ with their pagan world? How has anti-Christian persecution changed our modern world in the last decade? How does persecution from the ancient world and our modern world compare with the persecution in your world?

"Blessed are ye, when men shall say all manner of evil against you falsely for my sake." Gossip. Lies. Rumors. We hate them all. When those who hate God can't find anything bad to say about godly Christians, they start making things up. Remember, truth always wins. You can still be happy because you know your godly friends will never believe the lies and your ungodly enemies will never accept the truth.

Why should we be glad and rejoice for such persecution? First of all, you will have a great eternity! "For theirs is the kingdom of heaven . . . for great is your reward in heaven." We may be hated and persecuted for a short time here on earth, but never in heaven where time never ends.

You will be in great company! "For so persecuted they the prophets which were before you." Someday you may be able to sit and share your mutual stories of suffering with guys like Abel, Job, Joseph, Daniel, Paul, and even our Lord Jesus Christ. The suffering will be over and the glory will have just begun.

- Abel (Gen. 4:8)
- Job (Job 1:13–19)
- Joseph (Gen. 37:23–28; 39:20)
- Daniel (Dan. 6:16–17)
- Paul (2 Cor. 11:23–28)
- Jesus Christ (Isa. 53:1–7)

For I reckon that the sufferings of this present time are not worthy to be compared with the glory which shall be revealed in us. (Rom. 8:18)

Meditation 10

How can we create a thirst and hunger for God in others?

This is what God says.

Matthew 5:13–16

Ye are the salt of the earth: but if the salt have lost his savor, wherewith shall it be salted? It is thenceforth good for nothing, but to be cast out, and to be trodden under foot of men. Ye are the light of the world. A city that is set on an hill cannot be hid. Neither do men light a candle, and put it under a bushel, but on a candlestick; and it giveth light unto all that are in the house. Let your light so shine before men, that they may see your good works, and glorify your Father which is in heaven.

How can this affect me?

We are here on this earth for a reason.

- To show the world that there is a wonderful, powerful God who created our world and everything and everyone in it.
- To show the world that the guilt and conviction that we sense in our conscience is God's way of letting us know that we are all sinners in need of forgiveness.
- To show the world that God made a way for us to be reconciled to Him and forgiven through the sacrificial death of His Son, Jesus Christ.

When we fulfill God's intended purpose for our lives by letting God be in control and do "good" through us, we will be blessed.

When we insist on controlling our own lives and choose to do "evil" in defiance of God and His Word, we will be stressed.

A life crisis is not reserved for those approaching midlife. A stressful midlife (pre-mid or post-mid) crisis can happen to anyone at any time when that person realizes that he or she has lived most of life simply for personal pleasure and has accomplished nothing that pleases God or impacts others for eternity.

God's purpose is simple—glorify your Father who is in heaven. How? Jesus illustrates with two simple, but life-impacting illustrations.

Christian, you are the salt of the earth!

Salt needs to be salty! Once salt loses its ability to create thirst and hold back corruption it is worthless, good for nothing, fit only to be used as road fill. Salt needs to be salty. Believers need to believe. Christians need to be Christlike. Salty Christians are to hold back corruption and create a thirst for God.

Salt used to be extremely valuable. Some say that the word *salary* was derived from the word *salt* which was used to pay soldiers during the War of 1812.

> President Thomas Jefferson believed that Lewis and Clark would find an immensely valuable mountain of salt along the Missouri River.[1]

> There are over 14,000 uses for salt—if it is salty. If it is not, it is useless.[2]

Much of our saltiness is heard rather than seen. Colossians 4:6 and its parallel passage, Ephesians 4:29, give us a clue to the practical side of a salty testimony for Christ. Corrupt speech is abusive, cruel, and hurtful;

gracious speech is encouraging, thought provoking, and helpful.

> Let your speech be alway with grace, seasoned with salt, that ye may know how ye ought to answer every man. (Col. 4:6)

> Let no corrupt communication proceed out of your mouth, but that which is good to the use of edifying, that it may minister grace unto the hearers. (Eph. 4:29)

Christian, you are the light of the world!

Light cannot be hidden. The tiniest flicker of a flame can dispel total darkness in an instant. You cannot hide your light, and why would you want to? In our dark, dark world we need to use the light of our testimonies to draw attention to God. We want those trapped in their sinful darkness to see that we have a wonderful, forgiving, heavenly Father who will set them free.

Don't miss the word *cannot* in Matthew 5:14. If you are a true, believing believer (a salty Christian) who is walking with God, your light *will* be seen, attention *will* be drawn to God, and God *will* be glorified!

God has much to say about our lights shining brightly. Take a big breath and another sip of coffee, and meditatively read each passage below.

> But the path of the just is as the shining light, that shineth more and more unto the perfect day. (Prov. 4:18)

> For ye were sometimes darkness, but now are ye light in the Lord: walk as children of light: (for the fruit of the Spirit is in all goodness and righteousness and truth;) proving what is acceptable unto the Lord. And have no fellowship with the unfruitful works of darkness, but rather reprove them. For it is a shame even to speak of those things which are done of them in secret. But all things that are reproved are made manifest by the light: for whatsoever doth make manifest is light. Wherefore He saith, Awake thou that sleepest, and arise from the dead, and Christ shall give thee light. (Eph. 5:8–14)

> That ye may be blameless and harmless, the sons of God, without rebuke, in the midst of a crooked and perverse nation, among whom ye shine as lights in the world. (Phil. 2:15)

We are here on this earth for a reason.

Be salty. Shine brightly. You'll be blessed if you do.

Or be bland. Hide your light under a bushel, and you'll be stressed if you do.

Meditation 11

How can I ever be good
enough to go to heaven?

This is what God says.

Matthew 5:17–20

Think not that I am come to destroy the law, or the prophets: I am not come to destroy, but to fulfil. For verily I say unto you, Till heaven and earth pass, one jot or one tittle shall in no wise pass from the law, till all be fulfilled. Whosoever therefore shall break one of these least commandments, and shall teach men so, he shall be called the least in the kingdom of heaven: but whosoever shall do and teach them, the same shall be called great in the kingdom of heaven. For I say unto you, That except your righteousness shall exceed the righteousness of the scribes and Pharisees, ye shall in no case enter into the kingdom of heaven.

How can this affect me?

Trying to be perfect is quite stressful. Attempting to do everything just right all the time in every situation pushes our stress levels into the red. Perfection is actually an illusion for mere man. So why do we get so stressed over something that is impossible to achieve?

Comparisons can be dangerous unless we compare what our Lord is comparing—the righteousness of the scribes and Pharisees with our righteousness. If your righteousness and my righteousness does not exceed that of these religious leaders, we will never enter heaven. Ever!

Time to define. A clear understanding of our Lord's terms will help us.

Righteousness is holy, upright living, or doing right according to God's moral standard. The righteousness of the scribes and Pharisees was an external, hypocritical keeping of a list of laws, rules, and regulations. They looked good on the outside, but their hearts were filled with wickedness and self-centeredness. It was just a show. It was not too different from a school play where each character pretends to be something they are not. Actors are not portraying who they really are, but impress viewers to "think" they are who they are pretending to be. For these guys, life is a stage and nothing more.

True righteousness is an internal attitude-of-the-heart issue. Jesus was attacking those who outwardly looked like they were obeying the entire Old Testament law but were just pretending to be right with God. It is dangerous to pretend to be completely right with God when your heart is far from Him. The stress of others seeing the real you is frightening.

We, as sinners, are incapable of true righteousness. An awareness of our sinfulness should literally break our hearts and cause us to mourn before God. The more we mourn over our brokenness, the more we will hunger for God's righteousness. The righteousness that is better than that pretend righteousness of the religious leaders is a gift of God. We cannot earn it, work for it, pay for it, or be good enough to receive it. It is simply a gift of God to all who believe the gospel. Jesus Christ died for us, paid the penalty of sin for us, and gives—yes, freely credits—His righteousness to our accounts! Amen and amen.

Self-righteousness is simply an attempt to cover up selfishness and wickedness with lots and lots of good deeds, somehow believing that at whatever point our good outweighs our bad, we become good. God does not cover our sin, but does away with it through forgiveness and then freely imputes His righteousness to our accounts. Talk about stress-free living? Take a minute and slowly read each passage below three times. Then thank God for each truth from each phrase of His promises.

> Even the righteousness of God which is by faith of Jesus Christ unto all and upon all them that believe: for there is no difference: for all have sinned, and come short of the glory of God; being justified freely by his grace through the redemption that is in Christ Jesus. (Rom. 3:22–24)

> For with the heart man believeth unto righteousness; and with the mouth confession is made unto salvation. (Rom. 10:10)

> For he hath made him to be sin for us, who knew no sin; that we might be made the righteousness of God in him. (2 Cor. 5:21)

> I do not frustrate the grace of God: for if righteousness come by the law, then Christ is dead in vain. (Gal. 2:21)

And be found in him, not having mine own righteousness, which is of the law, but that which is through the faith of Christ, the righteousness which is of God by faith. (Phil. 3:9)

But after that the kindness and love of God our Savior toward man appeared, not by works of righteousness which we have done, but according to his mercy he saved us, by the washing of regeneration, and renewing of the Holy Ghost; which he shed on us abundantly through Jesus Christ our Saviour; that being justified by his grace, we should be made heirs according to the hope of eternal life. (Titus 3:4–7)

Abraham believed God, and it was imputed unto him for righteousness: and he was called the Friend of God. (James 2:23)

Meditation 12

If we are not right with others, we are not right with God.

This is what God says.

Matthew 5:21–26

Ye have heard that it was said by them of old time, Thou shalt not kill; and whosoever shall kill shall be in danger of the judgment: but I say unto you, That whosoever is angry with his brother without a cause shall be in danger of the judgment: and whosoever shall say to his brother, Raca, shall be in danger of the council: but whosoever shall say, Thou fool, shall be in danger of hell fire. Therefore if thou bring thy gift to the altar, and there rememberest that thy brother hath ought against thee; leave there thy gift before the altar, and go thy way; first be reconciled to thy brother, and then come and offer thy gift. Agree with thine adversary quickly, whiles thou art in the way with him; lest at any time the adversary deliver thee to the judge, and the judge deliver thee to the officer, and thou be cast into prison. Verily I say unto thee, Thou shalt by no means come out thence, till thou hast paid the uttermost farthing.

How can this affect me?

Knowing that you are not in a right relationship with God is stressful. Extremely stressful.

The stress of keeping right relationships with others sometimes seems like an impossibility. When we are at odds with others, we are at odds with God, and the pressure of both raises our stress levels from uncomfortable to unbearable. Jesus, through careful examination of this issue, offers some great counsel that we need to heed.

"Ye have heard . . . but I say." Jesus is not changing old laws here, but setting the laws straight. Religious leaders had added their thoughts to God's law for so long that it was hard to know the original law. It is always dangerous to mix man's opinions with God's Word.

Murder begins in the heart. Our Lord is describing and illustrating the righteousness that "exceeds the righteousness of the scribes and Pharisees" (Matt. 5:20). Remember, the kind of righteousness that pleases God begins in the heart. The Pharisee pretenders thought they were righteous because they had never murdered anyone. We have all heard of first-, second-, and third-degree murder, but here Jesus is teaching the three degrees of hatred that lead to a murderous heart.

- First-degree hatred: "Whosoever is angry with his brother without a cause."
- Second-degree hatred: "Whosoever shall say to his brother, Raca."
- Third-degree hatred: "Whosoever shall say, "Thou fool!""

Jesus said that those who call others names like *Raca* or *fool* would be in danger of severe judgment. *Raca* simply means "empty-headed," and *fool* is another name for an idiot or a moron. It is not these two names themselves, but the heart attitude of angrily belittling someone with utter disgust that is sin—sinful unrighteousness. Are you a name caller? Can you think of anyone who is still upset with you and offended because of what you said about them to others?

If you are not right with others, you are not right with God! Matthew 5:23 reminds us that if you go to worship, and while you are praying you remember that someone has "ought against" you (that is *anything* against you), stop praying and stop worshiping because God is not going to listen to you anyway.

So follow God's counsel in two ways.

- Be willing to settle your differences as quickly as possible by refusing to end the day with any issue unsettled.
- Be willing to forgive others in the same way that God has forgiven you.

God wants us to quickly settle our differences. If for whatever reason we cannot deal with them quickly, at least refuse to end the day with irreconcilable differences. Remember Paul's admonition in Ephesians 4:26–27? If you want to lessen your stress as you go to sleep at night, never go to bed angry.

> Be ye angry, and sin not: let not the sun go down upon your wrath: neither give place to the devil. (Eph. 4:26–27)

Forgiveness is a promise, and God never breaks a promise. When we confess, God forgives.

> If we confess our sins, he is faithful and just to forgive us our sins, and to cleanse us from all unrighteousness. (1 John 1:9)

Forgiveness is not a feeling, it is a promise. We can learn to forgive others in the same way that God forgives us.

> Be ye kind one to another, tenderhearted, forgiving one another even as God for Christ's sake hath forgiven you. (Eph. 4:32)

When you are right with others, you can be right with God.

When you are right with God, the stress seems to float away.

Meditation 13

Purity is an attitude that begins in the heart.

This is what God says.

Matthew 5:27–32

Ye have heard that it was said by them of old time,
Thou shalt not commit adultery: but I say unto you,
That whosoever looketh on a woman to lust after
her hath committed adultery with her already in his
heart. And if thy right eye offend thee, pluck it out,
and cast it from thee: for it is profitable for thee that
one of thy members should perish, and not that thy
whole body should be cast into hell. And if thy right
hand offend thee, cut it off, and cast it from thee:
for it is profitable for thee that one of thy members
should perish, and not that thy whole body should
be cast into hell. It hath been said, Whosoever
shall put away his wife, let him give her a writing
of divorcement: but I say unto you, That whosoever shall put away his wife, saving for the cause of

fornication, causeth her to commit adultery: and whosoever shall marry her that is divorced committeth adultery.

How can this affect me?

For some, maintaining physical and spiritual purity is one of the greatest stressors in life. Because it is a challenge that at times seems unattainable and insurmountable, way too many give up and give in without a fight.

Many cherish purity too little and love lust too much. We do what we love. We will please who we love the most. Again, purity is an issue that is dealt with in the heart.

Our Lord continues to describe the internal, God-given righteousness that exceeds "the righteousness of the scribes and Pharisees" (Matt. 5:20). A pharisaical attitude is driven more by duty than devotion. They try to do right because they *have to* in order to please men, rather than because they *want to* in order to please God. The Pharisee pretenders thought they were righteous because they had never technically committed adultery. Jesus reveals their impure hearts in the passage we are meditating on today.

- They pretended to be pure, but still lusted in their hearts after women. (Matt. 5:27–30)
- They pretended to be pure, but permitted divorce for all kinds of silly reasons so that they could then marry those they lusted after. (Matt. 5:31–32)
- They pretended to be pure, but still made promises and commitments that they knew they would break and not keep. (Matt. 5:33–37)

How pure is your heart before God? Do you struggle with lust? Are you willing to be committed to the biblical mandate of one woman for one man for one lifetime? Do you keep the promises you make without looking for ways to get out of them?

How can you consistently maintain purity in your thoughts, purity in your commitments, and purity in your word?

To maintain purity of thought, Jesus illustrates with some vivid and radical illustrations. He is not teaching self-mutilation here, but is showing the importance of a pure life in contrast to the consequences of an impure life. All of us know individuals whose lives have been devastated by porn enslavement, infidelity, and sexual addictions.

Most who have given into the flesh feel like losers. Talk about stress. Because many choose impurity over purity, they choose the stress of rejection, the stress of constant failure, the stress of hopeless entrapment, the stress of losing their family, and more, over living a life of forgiveness, purity, and consistent spiritual victory. How many times do we need to repeat a sin before it is a life-dominating sin? I don't know, and I really don't want to find out.

Consistent victory in the area of moral purity involves a combination of personal heartfelt brokenness, a complete and utter God-dependence, and a saturation of heart and mind with the Word of God. We are reminded in 1 Corinthians 6:9–11 that as believers in Christ we can be washed, sanctified, and justified through God's Holy Spirit. Victory and cleansing can be experienced.

> Know ye not that the unrighteous shall not inherit the kingdom of God? Be not deceived: neither fornicators, nor idolaters, nor adulterers, nor effeminate, nor abusers of themselves with mankind, nor thieves, nor covetous, nor drunkards, nor revilers, nor extortioners, shall inherit the kingdom of God. And such were some of you: but ye are washed, but ye are sanctified, but ye are justified in the name of

the Lord Jesus, and by the Spirit of our God. (1 Cor. 6:9–11)

Hebrews 13:4–5 is a comforting passage that shows us that the enemy of immoral covetousness (desiring that which God never intended us to have) is a contented heart that recognizes that God is more than enough and that as we live in His constant presence we can never hide from God (and why would we want to).

> Marriage is honorable in all, and the bed undefiled: but whoremongers and adulterers God will judge. Let your conversation be without covetousness; and be content with such things as ye have: for he hath said, "I will never leave thee, nor forsake thee." (Heb. 13:4–5)

First Timothy 1:5 expresses the trap many can fall into: pretending that you are pure, have a clean conscience, and are walking with God, when in reality the squeaky-clean public life is just a cover-up of wretched, raunchy private lives. When you tie these three passages together it reminds us of the greatest of all commandments in Matthew 22:36–39. Believers who have been transformed by God's wonderful salvation must focus on loving God (1 Cor. 6:9–11) and loving others (1 Tim. 1:5) rather than loving self. We will always do what we love the most. We will always please who we love the most.

> Now the end of the commandment is charity [love] out of a pure heart, and of a good conscience, and of faith unfeigned [no pretending]. (1 Tim. 1:5)

Meditation 14

"I promise—and my fingers are not crossed."

This is what God says.

Matthew 5:33–37

Again, ye have heard that it hath been said by them of old time, Thou shalt not forswear thyself, but shalt perform unto the Lord thine oaths: but I say unto you, Swear not at all; neither by heaven; for it is God's throne: nor by the earth; for it is his footstool: neither by Jerusalem; for it is the city of the great King. Neither shalt thou swear by thy head, because thou canst not make one hair white or black. But let your communication be, Yea, yea; Nay, nay: for whatsoever is more than these cometh of evil.

How can this affect me?

Keep your word. Guard your trust. Let your "yes" be "yes" and your "no" be "no." If your goal in life is to destroy all your close relationships, then simply break your promises. Mistrust is stressful to live with, whether others mistrust you or you mistrust others. Making a promise with your fingers crossed is simply a lie. Nobody loves being lied to. Actually, a broken promise is a bold-faced lie. What does God say about your relationship with those you lie to?

> A lying tongue hateth those that are afflicted by it;
> and a flattering mouth worketh ruin. (Prov. 26:28)

Never trust Satan to keep a promise. He promises joy and gives regrets. He promises satisfaction and gives disappointment. He promises pleasure and gives nothing but guilt. The only thing that Satan is good at is breaking his promises. Remember Goliath? Satan's bully? He promised, "Choose a man for yourselves, and let him come down to me. If he is to fight with me and kill me, then we will be your servants!" (1 Sam. 17:8–10 NKJV) Lie! The minute this God-hating beast fell to the ground and lost his head, the Philistines fled.

Satan loves to lie. Satan hates the truth. Jesus reminds the promise-breaking religious leaders, "Ye are of your father the devil, and the lusts of your father ye will do. He was a murderer from the beginning, and abode not in the truth, because there is no truth in him. When he speaketh a lie, he speaketh of his own: for he is a liar, and the father of it" (John 8:44).

When a Pharisee made a promise by swearing *by heaven*, *by earth*, *by Jerusalem*, or *by* their own *heads*, to them, it was like making a promise with their fingers crossed. They would say what needed to be said to look good, but never intended to follow through with what they promised.

How important is trust in relationships? In marriage commitments? In borrowing money? In showing up for work? In sharing your heart with friends? Without trust promises are worthless and stressful relationships multiply.

Managing trust is like managing a bank account. The more trust you put into your account, the more secure and satisfied are those loved ones and friends who have learned to trust you. When you deceive or disappoint those who trust you through selfishness and sin, you withdraw from that account. We need to remember that some sinful acts are so grievous and hurtful that they can literally bankrupt your entire account. When that happens, it does not need to be the end of those relationships. Just like a bank account, you can make deposits and regain trust through humble repentance and consistent change. This takes time. This takes grace-producing determination. But your trust account can grow once again and relationships can be reconciled.

God never breaks a promise. When He promises strength, He will deliver. When God promises to provide for us, we will never go without. When God promises to love us, He never changes His mind.

> Finally, my brethren, be strong in the Lord, and in the power of His might. (Eph. 6:10)

> But my God shall supply all your need according to His riches in glory by Christ Jesus. (Phil. 4:19)

> Nay, in all these things we are more than conquerors through Him that loved us. For I am persuaded, that neither death, nor life, nor angels, nor principalities, nor powers, nor things present, nor things to come, nor height, nor depth, nor any other creature, shall be able to separate us from the love of God, which is in Christ Jesus our Lord. (Rom. 8:37–39)

Meditation 15

Genuine believers and mere professors are different.

This is what God says.

Matthew 5:38–48

Ye have heard that it hath been said, An eye for an eye, and a tooth for a tooth: but I say unto you, That ye resist not evil: but whosoever shall smite thee on thy right cheek, turn to him the other also. And if any man will sue thee at the law, and take away thy coat, let him have thy cloke also. And whosoever shall compel thee to go a mile, go with him twain. Give to him that asketh thee, and from him that would borrow of thee turn not thou away.

Ye have heard that it hath been said, Thou shalt love thy neighbour, and hate thine enemy. But I say unto you, Love your enemies, bless them that curse you, do good to them that hate you, and pray for them which despitefully use you, and persecute you; that ye may be the children of your Father which is in heaven: for he maketh his sun to rise on the evil and on the good, and sendeth rain on the just and on the unjust. For if ye love them which love you, what reward have ye? do not even the publicans the same? And if ye salute your brethren only, what do ye more than others? do not even the publicans so? Be ye therefore perfect, even as your Father which is in heaven is perfect.

How can this affect me?

People are stressful. Some are full of stress and some fill others with stress. People are stressful.

You don't have to look too far to find grumpy, grouchy, greedy individuals. This is not a partial list of the seven dwarfs; it is a realistic list of selfish people who live by the pharisaical "eye for an eye, tooth for a tooth" way of life instead of the Christlike "turn the other cheek, go the extra mile" way.

From genuine believers, Christ expects a loving attitude even when we are unloved and treated unfairly.

The hypocritical scribes and Pharisees had twisted the original law by not only allowing a vengeful spirit of retaliation "an eye for an eye, and a tooth for a tooth" (Matt. 5:38), but also by deleting the phrase "as yourself" from "Thou shalt love your neighbor" (Lev. 19:18) and adding "hate thine enemy" to the law, which is no-where to be found in Scripture. Mere professors love to twist the Bible to make it say what they want it to say. They forget that the Word of God is unchangeable and the consequences of disobedience are unavoidable.

Our stress levels rise quickly when Dr. Angry hits us (Matt. 5:39), Miss Greedy sues us (5:40), Mr. Lazy compels or forces us to do something we'd rather not do (5:41), or Mrs. Discontent asks us to loan her money (5:42).

Slowly read Matthew 5:46–47 again. What do you think the phrases "What reward have ye?" and "What do ye more than others?" mean?

Our Lord expects much more from genuine believers than from those who profess to know God but really do not know Him. People can peek into our hearts by simply watching us respond to prickly people. What we do shows what we really are. What we say shouts what our true character really looks like. The Pharisee way resists others and treats them the same evil way that they were treated. The godly way returns good for evil. Which is an easier way to live? Which way takes more maturity, patience, and understanding? Which way shows Christlike character? Which way shows Christlike love? Which way did Christ live? Which way do you live?

From genuine believers, Christ expects a patient attitude even when we are tempted to be hateful and unloving toward those who are hateful and unloving to us.

So how do you deal with the stress of being:

- Regarded as an enemy
- Cursed as a nobody
- Hated as a worthless nothing
- Spitefully viewed as useless and insignificant

You do what genuine children of God would do:

- Love
- Bless
- Do good
- Pray

Children often imitate their fathers—the way they walk, talk, and interact with others. We can prove to others that we really are God's children by imitating His love toward both the evil and good—the just and unjust.

God loves His created beings. His love and tenderness is conspicuous in every sunrise and each rain shower. How conspicuous is your love for the prickly people who consistently bring more stress into your life?

"For God so loved the world" (John 3:16), and so should we.

Part *Two*

What Does Christ Ask Us to *Do* to Stress Less and Trust More?

Meditation 16

Be real. Life is not a one-act play.

This is what God says.

Matthew 6:1–5

Take heed that ye do not your alms [give to the needy] before men, to be seen of them: otherwise ye have no reward of your Father which is in heaven. Therefore when thou doest thine alms [give to the needy], do not sound a trumpet before thee, as the hypocrites do in the synagogues and in the streets, that they may have glory of men. Verily I say unto you, They have their reward. But when thou doest alms, let not thy left hand know what thy right hand doeth: that thine alms may be in secret: and thy Father which seeth in secret himself shall reward thee openly. And when thou prayest, thou shalt not be as the hypocrites are: for they love to pray standing in the synagogues and in the corners of the streets, that they may be seen of men. Verily I say unto you, They have their reward.

Moreover when ye fast, be not, as the hypocrites, of a sad countenance: for they disfigure their faces, that they may appear unto men to fast. Verily I say unto you, They have their reward. But thou, when thou fastest, anoint thine head, and wash thy face; that thou appear not unto men to fast, but unto thy Father which is in secret: and thy Father, which seeth in secret, shall reward thee openly.

How can this affect me?

Do you want to trust more and stress less? Be real. Be yourself. Don't get stressed out by trying to be someone or something that you are not. Don't get stressed by fearing that someone will reveal the real you. Just be you!

You can't fake true humility. You can pretend to be rich; you can pretend to be important; you can pretend to be spiritual; you can pretend that everything is fine; but you cannot pretend to impact lives for Christ and eternity.

Be real before God and you can be real before men. Bible commentator John MacArthur had this to say about the Greek word *theaomai* which is translated in Matthew 6:1 with the phrase "to be seen of men."

> [The word] *theaomai* (to be noticed) is . . . a spectacle
> to be gazed at. . . . Jesus is warning about practic-
> ing a form of righteousness . . . whose purpose is to
> show off before men. Such religion is like a play; it
> is not real life but acting. It does not demonstrate
> what is in the minds and hearts of the actors, but is
> simply a performance designed to make a certain
> impression on those who are watching. Such prac-
> tices amount to theatrical righteousness, performed
> to impress, rather than serve and to magnify the
> actors, rather than God. The purpose is to please
> men, not God, and the activities are not real life but
> an exhibition.[1]

Hypocrites live a life of stress. It is hard to keep your balance while walking on a picket fence. One false step . . . ouch! The stress escalates with the turmoil of knowing which side of the fence you want to land on. People pleasers are poor fence straddlers because there are people on both sides of the fence that they want to please. Once the hypocrite realizes that those on both sides of the fence are laughing at those who try to live in two worlds at the same time, they are stressed even more.

Why would anyone pretend to be right with God when they are not? Ask yourself. Do you desire for others to think that you are something that you wish you were, but are not? Do you want others to think you are committed to the Word of God, but seldom have consistent devotions? Do you want others to believe that you are a prayer warrior, but rarely find time to fervently pray? Do you attempt to portray the life of a religious, righteous, respectable child of God, but have a heart that is full of fear, envy, strife, contention, anger, and bitterness?

Examine your motives. Check your heart and ask the big "why." Why do you want to be something that you are not? If it is for others to accept you or be awed with your greatness, forget it. God is not in the habit of feeding our selfishness. If God's Spirit is truly convicting you, and your desire for change is focused on pleasing God and not men, then God will enable you to stop your hypocritical play, rewrite the script, and by His grace start being real.

Three times in our meditation passage Jesus says, "Truly I say to you, they have their reward" (6:2, 5, 16 NASB). In others words, that is all they get. Their giving, praying, and fasting gains the temporary admiration of men. We are certainly shortsighted when we forgo the eternal reward that God offers and crave the praise of men who will forget about us tomorrow. Wouldn't you rather God's eternal smile than the momentary applause of men?

There are three ways to wrestle with the thought, "I want everyone to think that I am something that I wish I was, but am not!"

1. Don't look for the easy way out. Change takes effort. There are no pills to take or lightning bolts to zap zeal into your heart. Don't think others have it any easier than you. God's method of change is the same for all of us, and it involves effort on our part and efficacious grace on God's part.

2. Examine your wish list. If each item on your wish list involves internal character and not external appearance or giftedness, by God's grace you can change and become the person you wish to be. Remember, true transformation and change is a result of a renewed mind. Let your holy God through His holy Word make you holy, as He is holy.

3. Study yourself. Know yourself. Accept who you are and how God made you; be thankful

for the gifts and abilities that God has already given you; don't pursue gifts that are not yours to be had; be *you* for the glory of God!

Those who are selfish in secret (their private lives) are quick to put on their masks in public! Meditate on what our Lord said about pretentious living in the verses listed below and note the thinking which drives this world of pretenders to clamor for the stage "to be seen of men."

> Nevertheless among the chief rulers also many believed on him; but because of the Pharisees they did not confess him, lest they should be put out of the synagogue: for they loved the praise of men more than the praise of God. (John 12:42–43)

> But all their works they do for to be seen of men. (Matt. 23:5)

> Woe unto you, scribes and Pharisees, hypocrites! for ye devour widows' houses, and for a pretence make long prayer: therefore ye shall receive the greater damnation. (Matt. 23:14)

Meditation 17

Retake Prayer 101.

This is what God says.

Matthew 6:5–13

And when thou prayest, thou shalt not be as the hypocrites are: for they love to pray standing in the synagogues and in the corners of the streets, that they may be seen of men. Verily I say unto you, They have their reward. But thou, when thou prayest, enter into thy closet, and when thou hast shut thy door, pray to thy Father which is in secret; and thy Father which seeth in secret shall reward thee openly. But when ye pray, use not vain repetitions, as the heathen do: for they think that they shall be heard for their much speaking. Be not ye therefore like unto them: for your Father knoweth what things ye have need of, before ye ask Him. After this manner therefore pray ye: Our Father which art in heaven, Hallowed be Thy name. Thy kingdom come. Thy will be done in earth, as it is in heaven. Give us this day our daily bread. And forgive us our debts, as we forgive our debtors. And lead us not into temptation, but deliver us from evil: For thine is the kingdom, and the power, and the glory, for ever. Amen.

How can this affect me?

"When you pray." This is assumed for any believer seeking to deal with stress. Life's struggles are hard and self-made men usually experience self-made heart attacks because of the self-made stress they endure. Your stress level will go down when time in your prayer closet goes up. Luke reminds us of Jesus' admonition that men should always pray, and not faint, quit, throw in the towel, or give in to debilitating stress. (Luke 18:1)

"When you pray." For the busy man, taking time to pray is a chore. Even when he does pray, his prayer time ends up being a time of reflection on a checklist of what he needs to accomplish that day. Stress multiplies when our lives become too busy to talk to God.

"When you pray." Just the mere fact that you are reading this book tells me there are probably individuals in your life that assume that you pray. Your wife? Your husband? Your kids? Your parents? Your church friends? Would your list of assumers be pleased or disappointed if they really knew the extent and fervency of your prayer-closet-life? Even though our Lord breathed the words "when you pray" for Matthew to write, because of His omniscience He never assumes anything. He knows! An all-knowing God never assumes. He knows when you pray. He knows how you pray. He knows what you pray. He knows why you pray. He knows, because He is the only one in all the universe who can hear all of us (from our prayer closets all over the world) at the same time.

"Enter into your closet and shut the door." If you want to learn how to pray in public, practice in your closet first (with the door shut).

Why a closet? It is filled with clothes and shoes, which normally will not interrupt you. It is a quiet place with very few distractions (unless you are trying to decide what to wear while you are in there).

Why a closet? Most of our closets are big enough for only one person—that is, one person and God. The importance of getting alone with God is incalculable in the noisy, busy, hustling, bustling world that we live in. Most closets do not have big screen TVs or Internet access (as long as you make sure to leave your phone in another room). Remember, your "closet" does not have to be where you keep your clothes or store your shoes; it can be a study, the living room before anyone else is out of bed, or even your bedroom before life's demands begin pounding on your door.

"Shut the door!" By shutting the door of your closet you make a secret place even more secret by shutting out the world and being alone with God. The bottom line is to find a closet where you can spend some quiet, secret, undistracted time with God . . . and use it.

"Pray to your Father who is in secret." Once you have found your secret place to meet with God, you can share those secret things with God that only He and you know—and should ever know. It is OK to have some secrets with God. Don't advertise or emphasize them to others. Keep them a secret. Advertising the secret things you do for God could cause you to become pharisaical. Emphasizing the secret things you have experienced with God could make you appear proud. Keep your secrets with God. God is pleased when it is just you and Him that know about your secret worship.

"For they love to pray standing in the synagogues and in the corners of the streets," "they think that they shall be heard for their much speaking," and they use "vain repetitions." Be careful not to pray in public just to make others think that you pray in private. Be careful to remember that prayer is talking to God and not a means to impress others. Hopefully church leaders, pastors, Sunday school teachers, deacons, elders, and ushers are not only heard praying in church, but also at home.

Public prayer should simply be an outpouring or an overflowing of your private times alone with God.

Public praying can at times be anything but talking to God. Sometimes it is talking to others about God; sometimes it is a rehash of the message; sometimes it is an interlocked series of Christianized clichés that start with "thank you for this day" and end with a traditional "Amen." But sometimes it is a direct conversation with a living God that hushes the hearers as they sense that the one praying knows what it means to be in the presence of God. How does your private time with God influence your public prayers?

What we commonly call "The Lord's Prayer" is actually a model or a pattern of prayer that Jesus gave to His disciples at least two different times—once during His sermon preached from an unknown mountain (Matt. 5–7) and the other in response to one of His disciples asking Him, "Lord, teach us to pray" (Luke 11:1). The Lord's prayer is not really meant to be a child's prayer or a simplistic ritualistic prayer traditionally quoted by massive congregations. It is a prayer that was given to those who are committed to the cause of Christ's kingdom and are willing to live and die for Him.

The first requests deal with God and His glory. He is a living, heavenly Father whose name must be cherished and whose will must be desired. The second set of requests deals with our past, present, and future needs. Presently we need God's daily provision; we often need to seek forgiveness for our sin and selfishness in the recent past; and we always need God's grace and strength to face temptation in the future.

"Our Father, who art in heaven, hallowed be Thy name." Don't ever forget to whom you are praying and unintentionally use God's name in an unholy or vain way. Prayer is talking to God and not a spiritual duty designed to impress, inspire, or instruct others. While talking to God, we should have nothing in our hearts but God.

Our heavenly Father is "in" heaven! He is real. He is alive. He hears your fervent prayers when you desperately cry out to Him. Sad to say, but God also hears our incessant babbling of memorized, meaningless, religious phrases that way too often make their way into our prayers.

Jesus hints on how to approach God in prayer—"Our Father." If you have entered into a personal relationship with Jesus Christ as your personal Lord and Savior, then you know that prayer is centered around your personal relationship with your heavenly Father. Any child should have the liberty, and even the joy, of going to his or her father at any time with any need, any desire, and any care with the confidence that his or her father will come to the rescue with incalculable wisdom and never ending love. There is nothing more satisfying than a child approaching his father in love, admiration, and respect. God loves the same from His children—even you and me.

"Your kingdom come. Your will be done in earth" (on earth just like it is being done right now in heaven). Be consumed with God's will rather than your wants. As a citizen of heaven submit yourself to the government of heaven. Let Christ, the King of heaven, rule in your heart by faith. God's will is being done in heaven, will be done on earth for the thousand years of His millennial reign, and should be done in our hearts day by day by day.

"Give us this day our daily bread." Don't miss the word "us." Be others-focused in your prayer life: "give us," "forgive us," "lead us." Spend as much time praying for others as you do for yourself.

"This day . . . daily bread." God knows both the quantity of food and the quality of food that is necessary to keep us healthy. He knows what we need each day of our lives. The "this day" and "daily" are a reminder of God's presence, provision, and protection. Every time we eat we should be reminded of our God's spiritual food—His Word.

A contented heart thanks God for what He has given before it starts praying for more. Instead of "give me," it is "thank You."

"And forgive us our debts, as we forgive [have forgiven] our debtors." We are all debtors to God! Just think what He has done for us in our salvation. As believers, we have been forgiven. Because we are who we are (sinners), forgiveness is a daily need. Because God is who He says He is (Savior), His gracious, undeserved forgiveness has no end. A heart full of gratitude for God's forgiveness automatically trusts more and stresses less.

Commentator John MacArthur explains the need for daily forgiveness as illustrated in what is commonly called the "Last Supper" when Jesus washed the disciple's feet.

> During the Last Supper, Jesus began washing the disciples' feet as a demonstration of the humble, serving spirit they should have as His followers. At first Peter refused, but when Jesus said, "If I do not wash you, you have no part with Me," Peter went to the other extreme, wanting to be bathed all over. Jesus replied, "He who has bathed needs only to wash his feet, but is completely clean; and you are clean, but not all of you" For He knew the one who was betraying Him; for this reason He said, "Not all of you are clean"(John 13:5–11).

> Jesus' act of foot washing was therefore more than an example of humility; it was also a picture of the forgiveness God gives in His repeated cleansing of those who are already saved. Dirt on the feet symbolizes the daily surface contamination from sin that we experience as we walk through life. It does not, and cannot, make us entirely dirty, because we have been permanently cleansed from that.

The positional purging of salvation that occurs at regeneration needs no repetition, but the practical purging is needed every day, because every day we fall short of God's perfect holiness.

As Judge, God is eager to forgive sinners, and as Father He is even more eager to keep on forgiving His children. Hundreds of years before Christ, Nehemiah wrote, "Thou art a God of forgiveness, gracious and compassionate, slow to anger, and abounding in lovingkindness" (Nehemiah 9:17).[1]

"And lead us not into temptation, but deliver us from evil." Temptation is stressful. We are weak. We need help. We need an almighty protector to keep us far away from the Evil One. As God enables us to resist the Devil, the Devil runs and flees just as he did when God cast his proud and rebellious heart out of heaven. Satan does not fear us, but he certainly fears the one who has already defeated him.

Did you know that our dear Lord prayed for us in His great intercessory prayer?

I do not pray that You should take them out of the world, but that You should keep them from the evil one. (John 17:15 NKJV)

The word *deliver* (*rhúomai*) was used to describe a dangerous rescue mission where a soldier would sneak into enemy territory and drag a fellow soldier away from danger. "Lord, rescue us from the evil one."

"For Thine is the kingdom, and the power, and the glory, forever. Amen." Forever and forever, dear Lord, I want you to have absolute authority in my life. I want Your dynamic power to be evident in my life as I totally depend on You and Your strength. I want my life to glorify You—whether I eat, or drink, or whatever I do, I want to praise You for Your glorious perfection.

"Amen." So be it; truly; surely; certainly. Yes, yes, yes!

Meditation 18

Be forgiven. Be forgiving.

This is what God says.

Matthew 6:14–15

For if ye forgive men their trespasses, your heavenly Father will also forgive you: but if ye forgive not men their trespasses, neither will your Father forgive your trespasses.

How can this affect me?

I get all excited when I see a promise from God addressed personally to me. God never breaks a promise, He cannot lie, and He is always true to His word. If He promises it, I can believe it.

God promises me that if I am willing to forgive others, He is willing to forgive me. I constantly need His forgiveness, because I am constantly doing, saying, or thinking in ways that displease Him.

When I get an attitude and refuse to ask God for forgiveness, I am stressed. Really stressed. Guilt is a heavy burden to bear. Conviction is incredibly stressful. Knowing that my unconfessed sin causes me to be out of fellowship with God and puts me on no-speaking-terms with those I should love stresses me out. I know that God's forgiveness is not unconditional. If I refuse to forgive others, God refuses to forgive me. That's stressful. We all know this, but still we wrestle with foolish thoughts like these.

- "I'll never forgive him!"
- "I only hope that someone hurts her as much as she has hurt me."
- "I hate him!"
- "If he would just ask for forgiveness I would give it, but I know he never will."

I have to constantly remind myself that forgiveness is a promise, not a feeling. Since God keeps His promise to me, I must keep my promise to those I need to forgive. Forgiveness is a blessing to receive and a blessing to give. If I confess, God is faithful to forgive. I wish I could be as faithful to forgive others as God is to forgive me.

The more you understand and accept forgiveness, the more your love will grow for God and others. Really, just to know how much you are loved (and forgiven) makes a huge difference in your life.

> And be ye kind one to another, tenderhearted, forgiving one another, even as God for Christ's sake hath forgiven you. (Eph. 4:32)

Forgiveness is a promise, but it is not forgetting. The Scripture never says that God "forgets" our sins. When God says, "Their sins . . . will I remember no more" (Heb. 10:17), He is not forgetting; He has chosen to not remember or hold those sins against us ever again. God cannot forget because He is omniscient—all-knowing. God cannot forget because He is immutable—unchanging. He cannot increase or decrease in knowledge, therefore, He cannot forget. What He can do is to refuse to bring those sins to His mind against us ever again.

> There is therefore now no condemnation to them which are in Christ Jesus. (Rom. 8:1)

So if we are to obey Ephesians 4:32 and forgive others the same way that God has forgiven us, we can forgive others without feeling like it or forgetting what they did. We choose to forgive others the same way that God chooses to forgive us. This gives me hope. God did it for me, and by His grace I can do it for those who have sinned against me.

Forgiveness is the key that opens your own Pandora's box of past hurt, regret, abuse, pain, sorrow, spite, envy, hate, and more. When you forgive, you unlock that beat-up, old treasure chest you've been dragging around for years, and the bitter, selfish, hateful bats of your past will fly off into the heavens never to be seen again. Forgive and you will stress less.

> And be ye kind one to another, tenderhearted, forgiving one another, even as God for Christ's sake hath forgiven you. (Eph. 4:32)

> Forbearing one another, and forgiving one another, if any man have a quarrel against any: even as Christ forgave you, so also do ye. (Col. 3:13)

> Dearly beloved, avenge not yourselves, but rather give place unto wrath: for it is written, Vengeance is mine; I will repay, saith the Lord. Therefore if thine enemy hunger, feed him; if he thirst, give him drink: for in so doing thou shalt heap coals of fire on his head. Be not overcome of evil, but overcome evil with good. (Rom. 12:19–21)

Meditation 19

Keep your financial focus eternal.

This is what God says.

Matthew 6:19–21

Lay not up for yourselves treasures upon earth, where moth and rust doth corrupt [consume], and where thieves break through and steal: but lay up for yourselves treasures in heaven, where neither moth nor rust doth corrupt, and where thieves do not break through nor steal: for where your treasure is there will your heart be also.

How can this affect me?

We are inclined to become content with what we have, which will not last, and discontent with what we can have, which will last forever.

Financial pressures are stressful. Why do you think money struggles are among the top five reasons for divorce? Why is suicide often linked to financial loss? Why do money and stuff stress us out so much? Either we are stressed because we don't have enough and want more, or we are stressed because we have a lot and are afraid we are going to lose it. Either way, an improper view of finances is a sure-fire way to raise our stress levels to a fever pitch.

There are four words in Matthew 6:19–21 that sum up the way our Lord wants us to view money, investments, savings, and stuff: *not earth, but heaven.*

Say it out loud a couple times—*not earth, but heaven.* Our earthly treasures are temporal. Their shelf life is so fickle there is no promise they will still be there when we think we need them. When our lives end, the expiration date stamped on our earthly stockpile of stuff kicks in. Jesus reminds us to invest in heaven, which is eternal, rather than earth, which is temporal. Not earth, but heaven.

When I wanted to impress an English teacher with my massive vocabulary, I would secretly reach for a thesaurus, which, as you know, is an encyclopedia, or a treasury, of synonyms and antonyms. The root word for *lay up* and *treasures* comes from *thesaurós,* which means to store or treasure up goods for future use. The Lord is reminding us that it is foolish to "treasure up treasures" for ourselves! Stacking up coins, stockpiling gold, and hoarding every little penny will give you the heart of a Scrooge and the mind of Gollum. A bah-humbug attitude will keep you from giving, and a mind consumed with "My precious!" steals the joy of being a blessing to others.

If our treasures can rust, get a virus, go out of style, or get stolen, they are temporal, earthly treasures. Our responsibility to guard them, take care of them, and protect them puts constant stress on our lives.

If our treasures are deposited safely in God's treasury (thesaurus) and are therefore God's responsibility to guard, take care of, and protect, we can live stress free as we trust God to protect and take care of our treasures. So which investment plan makes the most sense to you?

Heavenly securities are guaranteed by the promise and power of an almighty, omnipotent God. Fort Knox has the most impregnable vault on earth. It is built out of granite, sealed behind a 22-ton door, located on a US military base, and watched over day and night by army units with tanks and Apache helicopter gunships. Since its construction in 1937, the treasures locked inside Fort Knox have included the US Declaration of Independence, the Gettysburg Address, three volumes of the Gutenberg Bible, and the Magna Carta. Heavenly securities protected and guarded by our heavenly Father are even more secure than anything in Fort Knox.

My treasures are those things that are precious, prized, and priceless—not just because of their intrinsic value but because of their iconic value to me. What is the one thing that, if it were taken away from you, would make you want to die? I hope that the first answer that crawled into your mind included your relationship with your Lord and your relationships with all your family members. Those relationships are eternal.

Whether you know it or not, you already have a number of mothproof, rustproof, burglarproof treasures in your heavenly treasure house.

- Caring angelic friends (Matt. 18:10; Luke 12:8; Heb. 1:14; Eccl. 4:9)
- A home—a place to live (John 14:1–2; 2 Cor. 5:1)
- Both a city and the country to enjoy (Heb. 11:16)

- Love—a close, loving relationship with Christ (John 17:24–26)
- Joy—pleasurable things to do and enjoy (Ps. 16:11)
- Music—singing, playing instruments, writing music (Rev. 8:7–13; 15:2)
- Work—no boredom, serving because we want to (Matt. 25:23; Rev. 7:15; 22:3)
- Laughing—in the kingdom of God you will laugh and leap for joy (Luke 6:21)
- Peace—everything is OK and will be OK (Luke 19:38; Phil. 4:7; Col. 3:15)
- Fulfilled promises of God to enjoy forever
  - a life that will never end (John 3:16)
  - a gift that will never be lost (John 6:37, 39)
  - a hand out of which I will never be snatched (John 10:28)
  - a love from which I shall never be separated (Rom. 8:39)
  - a calling that will never be revoked (Rom. 11:29)
  - a foundation that will never be destroyed (2 Tim. 2:19)
  - an inheritance that will never fade out (1 Peter 1:4, 5)

We certainly don't have time to cover all there is to say about personal financial plans. But there are a number of questions to ask and principles to ponder as you attempt to establish a financial balance in your life that reduces stress to its bare minimum.

- What is your standard of living?
- What is your standard of giving?
- What is your standard of saving?
- What is your view of debt?
- What do you own that brings added stress into your life?

Take a family trip to the dump! (Lines are short and the admission is free.) Look at the "treasures" that people paid for, fought over, opened as presents, went in debt for, and thought they couldn't live without. Consider an Amish man's advice, "Show me what thou dost need, and I will show thee how to live without it." Learn to budget. Seek counsel from a godly financial expert.

Scripture has much to say about our finances. Here is an index to a book that could be entitled *Six Bible Secrets for Financial Security*. Write your own financial philosophy based on these six biblical principles and watch the financial stress in your life begin to disappear.

- The Scrawny Cow Principle (Joseph in Gen. 37)
- The Tiny Little Ant Principle (Solomon in Prov. 6)
- The Get-Rich-Quick Principle (Paul in 1 Tim. 6)
- The Plenty-in-the-Barn Principle (Solomon in Prov. 3)
- The Just-Enough Principle (Agur in Prov. 30)
- The Give-to-Give-More Principle (Luke 6:38)

How much do you think about money, savings, investments, or things? Do you control your "stuff," or does your "stuff" control you?

You think about what you love.

> For where your treasure is, there will your heart be also. (Matt. 6:21)

When you keep your financial focus eternal, you will stress less and trust more.

Meditation 20

Decide who is boss in charge of your life.

This is what God says.

Matthew 6:24

No man can serve two masters: for either he will hate the one, and love the other; or else he will hold to the one [be loyal to], and despise [look down upon] the other. Ye cannot serve God and mammon [money or wealth].

How can this affect me?

Stuff causes stress. Those who have little are stressed over getting more, and those who have much are stressed to keep it. Material things have a way of controlling our thoughts, our money, and our time. The more stuff you have the more stress you have.

There are some Bible principles that are found only in black or white. There is no neutral. It is a love or hate relationship. There is no middle ground. If you are devoted to one, you must despise the other. Joshua put it this way, "Choose you this day whom you will serve" (Josh. 24:15). Ruth passionately said, "For wherever you go, I will go; and wherever you lodge, I will lodge; your people shall be my people, and your God, my God" (Ruth 1:16 NKJV). Elijah cried for all to hear, "How long halt ye between two opinions? if the Lord be God, follow Him" (1 Kings 18:21). Here in Matthew 6:24, our Lord Jesus Christ is mandating that we make up our minds whom we are going to serve.

"No [one] man." Not even one, no exceptions, no excuses, no exemptions, no exclusions—no one. You are either on or off, in or out. There are absolutely no exceptions even for the exceptional!

"Can serve." The English word *serve* does not seem to be radical enough to convey what the Lord is emphasizing here. The word refers to a master-owned slave. No one can be a slave to two owners. A slave in the time of Christ was nothing more than a living machine or a living tool over which the owner had complete control.

Such a slave had no rights of his own, no time of his own, and no say about his life. The one and only owner was the one and only controller of his life.

"Can serve two." A divided heart breeds divided loyalties; a double heart is unstable and ready to fall; a submissive servant cannot submit to two opposing masters. What do we know about a Matthew 22:37 servant who serves with his entire heart, soul, mind, and strength? He serves because he wants to and not because he has to. Trying to serve two at the same time is like being a knot at the center of a tug-of-war rope. You are pulled toward one side, then the other, back and forth with such tension and stress you are ready to break. It is tiring to hold on to both sides. It is frustrating to try.

"Masters." A master lord is a supreme lord, a sovereign king, and the one in charge. A master owner has complete ownership of that which belongs to him. A master electrician or mechanic has mastered his craft and has both the experience and the knowledge to do what is best in his field. Such mastery is deserving of respect and confidence. When we are willing to recognize who owns us, who is in charge, and who knows what is best for us, we are ready to acknowledge that our Lord

Jesus Christ is not only our wonderful Lord, but our magnificent Master also.

Who, or what, is the master or the boss in your life? Who, or what, controls your thoughts? Who, or what, is in charge of your schedule? Who, or what, calls the shots, gives the orders, and has the final word in your life? Who, or what, adds stress to your life or reduces stress in your life?

Some choose a *what* for a boss. Money. Entertainment. Toys. Popularity. Acceptance. Cell phones. Computers. These *whats* can quickly take charge of our lives if we are not careful.

Others choose a *who* for a boss. God. You. Others. This list is short, but too often God ends up in third place with you and your friends in the first and second place.

Stress escalates when your attitude toward the authority you reject begins to surface. Such attitudes hurt and grieve those they are directed toward. In other words, when you tell God or show God that He is not your Master and Lord, you are actually despising Him and, in a way, hating Him. As your love for yourself and your stuff increases, your love for God decreases. It will happen! God said so. And remember, to *despise* means to belittle, to look down on, or to treat as dirt. It is absurd for us creatures to look down on our Creator. It is foolish for the weak to despise the Almighty. It does not make sense, but it does create stress.

Stress de-escalates when you allow God to be God and express your heartfelt love and unquestioned loyalty to Him. When you love God with all your heart, soul, mind, and strength, you will have no problem submitting to His lordship.

Blame your refusals to yield to temptation on God, His Word, His Will, and His desire for His best for your life. Let others know that God is the one in charge (the boss) in your life and not you.

- "Want a beer?" "No thank you." "Why?" "There are a number of reasons, but I made a promise to God that I'd stay away from it, and I really don't want to displease God."

- "If you love me, you will!" "No, if I truly love you, I won't! And furthermore, since I know that God truly loves me and I do love Him, I've already given my body to God, and He has set the guidelines that I must abide by. Sorry to upset you, but no thanks."

- "Man, won't your God let you do anything?" "Well, not anything that is not best for me or that I'll regret forever."

Your loyalty and dependence is expressed in the words *hold to* (*antecho*), which encourage us to hold firmly, to cleave, to not let go! Get a grip! Your grip will be determined by how you value that which you are holding on to. If the object is important to you and means the world to you, you are not going to let go. If the object is worthless, has no value, and is basically trash to you, you will let go. How you value your relationship with your Lord and Savior will determine how tightly you hold on.

This principle has got to be one of the greatest "stress releasers" I can think of. Every temptation and every trial is a test of our love and our loyalty to our Lord. Let God be in control of your life. Let Him be boss. No one can serve two masters, so don't even try.

Insist on being in control of your life, and you will stress more and trust less.

Give God control of your life, and you will stress less and trust more.

Your choice.

Meditation 21

Don't worry. Just trust.

This is what God says.

Matthew 6:25, 31–32

Therefore I say unto you, Take no thought [don't worry] for your life, what ye shall eat, or what ye shall drink; nor yet for your body, what ye shall put on. Is not the life more than meat, and the body than raiment?

Therefore take no thought [don't worry], saying, What shall we eat? or, What shall we drink? or, Wherewithal shall we be clothed? (For after all these things do the Gentiles seek:) for your heavenly Father knoweth that ye have need of all these things.

How can this affect me?

The Lord is not telling us to stop thinking! "Take no thought" takes some "thought" to understand our

Lord's thoughts. Forethought is one gift that God has given to us but kept back from the birds and the flowers. Sparrows and lilies don't worry, and neither should we. Worry is stressful.

When you learn how to keep from being overwhelmed with anxiety and controlled by debilitating worry, you will have mastered the simple concept that Jesus is talking about here. "Take no thought." Don't worry. Refuse to allow what might happen tomorrow to paralyze you today.

Those who "take thought" are troubled, anxious, and feel as if they are being torn in two different directions. Their thoughts are monopolized by their heart's concerns. Simply stated, they are stressed!

What do you normally think about? If we could list all our thoughts for one 24-hour period, and then circle the ones that have the lion's share of our thinking for that one day, which from the list below would be circled on your list?

Work Related	Thanksgiving	Social Media
Worry	Lust	Complaining
Relationships	Love	Finances
Praising God	Bitterness	Gossip

| Discontent | Prayer | Entertainment |
| Bible Meditation | Serving | Encouraging Others |

Don't stress over the necessities of life! The world is consumed with eating, drinking, and looking good. Take ten minutes with a Google search, and you will see that there are thousands of Dunkin' Donuts, Pizza Huts, Starbucks, and Subways, so we don't have to worry about eating. Soft drink sales are in the billions worldwide, so we don't have to worry about what to drink. GAP, Aeropostale, and Old Navy sales are in the billions each year, so don't worry about clothes.

Don't worry. God, your Heavenly Father knows what you need!

> Be not ye therefore like unto them: for your Father knoweth what things ye have need of, before ye ask him. (Matt. 6:8)

Don't worry. God, your heavenly Father, cares!

> Casting all your care on him; for he careth for you. (1 Peter 5:7)

Give your care, your anxieties, and your worries to God. He cares!

Don't worry. God, with forethought, will never give you anything that will harm you but only that which will help you! God is not into giving snakes and stones.

> "If a son asks for bread from any father among you, will he give him a stone? Or if he asks for a fish, will he give him a serpent instead of a fish? Or if he asks for an egg, will he offer him a scorpion? If you then, being evil, know how to give good gifts to your children, how much more will your heavenly Father give the Holy Spirit to those who ask Him!" (Luke 11:11–13 NKJV)

Why do we worry when we know that our heavenly Father cares and promises to meet our needs?

Worry is a sin that Christians commit perhaps more frequently than any other. Worry declares our heavenly Father, His Word, and His promises to be untrustworthy. Worry is not a trivial sin, because it attacks both God's love and God's integrity. Take no thought! Don't worry. You must just trust!

Don't stress. You will always get what you need, even though you may not always know what you need.

> But my God shall supply all your need according to his riches in glory by Christ Jesus. (Phil. 4:19)

Let's finish our meditation on stressful worry with a word from Charles H. Spurgeon. Stress and worry were even a problem back in the 1800s.

> Care, even though exercised upon legitimate objects, if carried to excess, has in it the nature of sin. The precept to avoid anxious care is earnestly inculated [taught] by our Saviour, again and again; it is reiterated by the apostles; and it is one which cannot be neglected without involving transgression: for the very essence of anxious care is the imagining that we are wiser than God, and the thrusting ourselves into his place to do for him that which He has undertaken to do for us. . . . Anxious care often leads to acts of sin. He who cannot calmly leave his affairs in God's hand, but will carry his own burden, is very likely to be tempted to use wrong means to help himself. This sin leads to a forsaking of God as our counselor, and resorting instead to human wisdom. . . . Anxiety makes us doubt God's lovingkindness, and thus our love to him grows cold. . . . Thus want of confidence in God leads us to wander far from him; but if through simple faith in his promise, we cast each burden as it comes upon him, and are "careful for nothing" because he undertakes to care for us, it will keep us close to him, and strengthen us against much temptation. "Thou wilt keep him in perfect peace whose mind is stayed on thee, because he trusteth in thee."[1]

Meditation 22

Build a bird feeder.

This is what God says.

Matthew 6:26

Behold the fowls of the air: for they sow not, neither do they reap, nor gather into barns; yet your heavenly Father feedeth them. Are ye not much better than they?

How can this affect me?

Build a bird feeder. Join a birdwatcher's club! Study closely the eagerness of the little yellow finches, the boldness of the cardinals, and the humility of the mourning doves. (Watch your cat watch the birds!)

As our Lord continues to deal with the stress of anxiety, fear, and worry, He illustrates with a common, everyday happening in most of our lives—eating and drinking. He reminds us in the previous verse (6:25) not to worry about what we will eat or drink. Spend a day watching birds and you will be reminded of God's comforting protection and constant provision. Really, don't stress. God will provide. God will protect.

Look at the birds! "Behold the fowls of the air." I think God is a birdwatcher. For centuries the sky above Palestine has been a haven for all kinds of birds. Moses must have spent some time watching birds as can be assumed in his list of twenty of them in Leviticus 11:13–19—the eagle, ossifrage, osprey, kite, falcon, raven, ostrich, nighthawk, sea gull, hawk, owl, cormorant, ibis, water hen, pelican, vulture, stork, heron, hoopoe, and bat. David talks about a sparrow and the swallow in Psalm 84:3. Even the barnyard birds are not neglected. Remember the beautiful passage about the hen and her chicks (Matt. 23:37), the rooster in Peter's denial (Matt. 26:34), and the dove in the baptism of Jesus (Matt. 3:16)? If God so notices the birds, do you really think that you, as His child, can go unnoticed?

"They neither sow, nor reap, nor gather into barns." Imagine an eagle driving a John Deere tractor or a couple of old owls and white doves baling hay! Now this is not to say that they are lazy. Birds are forever rushing around looking for food, finding just the right materials for their nests, protecting their eggs, and feeding their young. God's protection and provision in the bird world actually started when He created each little winged creature.

To understand and marvel at God's infinitesimal creativity, take a few minutes to Google some of God's most interesting creatures from the bird kingdom. Research to see whether the bald eagle is really bald; find out how fast an ostrich can run; study how many times a minute a hummingbird's heart actually beats; and investigate why many think that the sparrow is an incredibly annoying bird. Jesus Himself reminds us that we are more valuable than a pesky, little sparrow.

> Are not two sparrows sold for a copper coin? And not one of them falls to the ground apart from your Father's will. But the very hairs of your head are all numbered. Do not fear therefore; you are of more value than many sparrows. (Matt. 10:29–31 NKJV)

> [Note: Luke 12:6–7 offers a better deal—five sparrows for two copper coins.]

God has given us the ability and the knowledge to grow and gather food. The birds cannot take things into their own hands (they don't have hands), so they must trust or die. We must trust *and* work with the abilities that God has given us. God can and will work miracles through our feeble efforts. A widow woman made cakes for Elijah (and God kept the almost empty pots full); a little boy's mother prepared a lunch of five loaves and two fish (and God fed thousands with the lunch); servants filled water pots with water (and God turned the water into wine). We are to do what God has enabled us to do . . . and then watch God do what only He can do.

"Your heavenly Father feeds them. Are you not of more value than they?"

Commentators Hendriksen and Kistemaker state it so well.

> Christ's argument . . . If the birds, who cannot in any real sense plan ahead, have no reason to worry, then certainly you, my followers, endowed with intelligence, so that you can take thought for the future, should not be filled with apprehension. Again, if God provides even for these lower creatures, how much more will He care for you, who were created as His very image. And especially, if the One who feeds them is "*your heavenly Father*" but *their Creator*, then how thoroughly unreasonable your

anxiety becomes. "*You are of more value than they, are you not?*" asks the Lord, in a question so worded in the original that it expects an affirmative answer.[1]

So build a bird feeder. Watch how God protects and provides for each little creature. Thank God for His protection and provision in your life.

If you do, your stress will take on wings and fly away—just like a little bird.

Meditation 23

Relax. There are some things you cannot change.

This is what God says.

Matthew 6:27

Which of you by taking thought can add one cubit unto his stature?

How can this affect me?

Except for your stress level, nothing can be changed by worry. Anxious thoughts keep your stress at the top rung of the ladder as you focus on the things in life you don't like and want to change, but can't. Don't worry. Relax. There are some things you cannot change.

Trust and worry do not get along. By accepting what you cannot change, you are forced to trust God. The more you trust, the less you worry. Trust more. Stress less.

The word *stature* refers to *full age* and could be a bit confusing in this biblical context. Sometimes the word *stature* refers to *height* (how tall you will be at full age), and other times it refers to *lifespan* (how old you will be at full age). Either way you view this, it still illustrates something that is totally out of our control. Stressing about your age or height accomplishes absolutely nothing. Whether you want to be taller or live longer, both are in God's hands. Worry and stress can change nothing.

Which of you by worry can add eighteen inches to your height?

How tall would you like to be? When I play basketball, I want to be 6'8". When I have to squeeze into that window seat on my next flight, I like being 5'9". But think about it. Do I really want to add a cubit to my height? I am 5'9" and by adding a cubit I would be a 7'7" giant! I would constantly be stared at; I'd have a tough time fitting into most cars; it would be hard to find clothes to fit; I would bump my head on most doorways; it would be miserable!

Most short people desire to be taller (just check out the heels some girls wear). Zacchaeus dealt with his lack of height by climbing a tree in order to see Jesus. According to what we see in archeology, David was probably between 5'2" and 5'8", and the empty tomb near Jerusalem would suggest that Jesus himself was probably about 5'6". Neither would be impressive heights in our sports world today. David, Jesus, and you are the exact height that God's DNA blueprints predetermined.

Who of you, by being worried (anxious), can (has the power, the ability, or is able to) add a single hour to your life (as a full-aged adult)?

Not many want to die young. Most don't want to die old! Who does not want to live forever? We know that God promises everlasting life to those who trust the gospel message. Eternal life is promised to those whose sins have been forgiven and covered by the death of our wonderful Savior, Jesus Christ.

Although there is no expiration date on our birth certificates, we are reminded that life is short. The little dash (–) between our birthdate and the date of death inscribed on our tombstone represents the number of years that God graciously gives us. The dash is small—almost insignificant.

David, Job, and James all understood the brevity of life and knew that no one's life could be lengthened by worry, anxiety, or stress.

> Indeed, You have made my days as handbreadths, and my age is as nothing before You; certainly every man at his best state is but vapor. (Ps. 39:5 NKJV)

> Now my days are swifter than a runner; they flee away, they see no good. They pass by like swift ships, like an eagle swooping on its prey. (Job 9:25–26 NKJV)

> Whereas you do not know what will happen tomorrow. For what is your life? It is even a vapor that appears for a little time and then vanishes away. (James 4:14 NKJV)

You can worry yourself to death, but not to life. Dr. Charles Mayo, of the famous Mayo Clinic, wrote,

> "Worry affects the circulation, the heart, the glands and the whole nervous system. I have never met a man or known a man to die of overwork, but I have known a lot who died of worry."[1]

If I worry because I look like a squatty body, I cannot worry myself taller. If I am troubled and anxious because I might die young, I cannot worry more hours or days to my life.

Worry is senseless. Anxiety makes no sense. Being stressed out about something that we cannot change is nonsense. Rather than trying to change everything to our own liking, we must somehow and someday accept all difficult situations and difficult people from God without giving Him a deadline to remove them. It is much better to raise our patience levels than our stress levels.

Can you list even one positive consequence to worry and anxiety? Worry will accomplish absolutely nothing! Jesus said so!

> God grant me the serenity
> to accept the things I cannot change,
> the courage to change the things I can,
> and the wisdom to know the difference.[2]

Meditation 24

Stop and smell the lilies.

This is what God says.

Matthew 6:28–30

And why take ye thought for raiment? Consider the lilies of the field, how they grow; they toil not, neither do they spin: and yet I say unto you, That even Solomon in all his glory was not arrayed like one of these. Wherefore, if God so clothe the grass of the field, which to day is, and to morrow is cast into the oven, shall He not much more clothe you, O ye of little faith?

How can this affect me?

Do you stress over your appearance? Are you consumed with clothes? Do you stare in the mirror morning after morning wondering if others will think you are attractive and look good?

Most stress can be reduced through careful study. When God encourages us to *consider* anything, He wants us to slow down, take notice, and carefully study what He wants us to learn. In this case, wildflowers. Stopping and smelling the lilies is a great way to reduce stress.

Field lilies are simply wild, untamed flowers that grow with seemingly no effort. Without the help of an artist, a seamstress, or a florist, they are absolutely beautiful! Without any worth but that of fuel to be burned up in a wood stove, they are more attractive, more elegant, and more pristine than any garment King Solomon or anyone in his court would wear.

If God makes a field of weeds so beautiful, will He not take care of us?

How consumed are you with your appearance? How much time do you spend each morning preparing to be seen by your world of friends? How much money do you budget to "style"? How often do you complain saying, "I don't have anything to wear," only to find enough clothes in your closet to clothe a Third-World country?

Does your outward appearance receive more attention than your inward appearance? Consider the lilies, but also consider God's emphasis on appearance throughout the Bible. If you simply consider what God asks you to consider, I promise you will stress less and trust more.

Consider what the Lord told Samuel.

> Do not look at his appearance or at his physical stature . . . for the Lord does not see as man sees; for man looks at the outward appearance, but the Lord looks at the heart. (1 Sam. 16:7 NKJV)

Consider how Peter encouraged the ladies in his ministry to keep their appearance a heart issue.

> "Do not let your adornment be merely outward—arranging the hair, wearing gold, or putting on fine apparel—rather let it be the hidden person of the heart, with the incorruptible beauty of a gentle and quiet spirit, which is very precious in the sight of God. (1 Peter 3:3–4 NKJV)

Consider Peter's admonition to be clothed with "humility" (1 Peter 5:5) and Paul's encouragement to "put on" mercy, kindness, humility, meekness, patience, forbearance, forgiveness, and love (Col. 3:12–14).

Consider Jesus. According to Isaiah, "He hath no form nor comeliness; . . . there is no beauty that we should desire Him" (Isa. 53:2).

Consider the lilies.

Meditation 25

Prioritize. First things first.

This is what God says.

Matthew 6:33

But seek ye first the kingdom of God, and his right-eousness; and all these things shall be added unto you.

How can this affect me?

"But" instead of worrying about things today that you will forget about tomorrow, "but" rather than eagerly seeking and desiring food, drink, and clothes like those do who do not know Christ and have nothing else to live for, "but" in place of craving the things your heavenly Father already knows you need, seek first, prioritize, and concentrate on God's kingdom and God's righteousness. Focus your attention on the things of the

Lord, and everything that you are prone to worry about, eagerly seek, or crave (the things God already knows you need) will be added to what you already have been given by God. God will take care of you.

Did you know that you can prioritize stress right out of your life? The famous idiom "Don't get the cart before the horse" simply means to do things in their proper order. First things first. Whether motivated by laziness or impatience, we often want the end result without taking the effort or the time to achieve that result. We worry and stress over getting what God has already promised He would give us. It does not make a lot of sense.

We say, "Let me take care of my needs first—I want to be well fed and look good—and then I'll see if I have time for God." God says, "If you diligently seek to submit to My authority in My kingdom and passionately search for the only righteousness that will truly please Me, then I promise I will take care of every need in your life."

Seeking God's kingdom and God's righteousness is our twofold, number one thing to do. When you submit to God's authority and let His Spirit control your life, you will do right. You will do right joyfully. You will do right with a calm confidence and a satisfying peace that is almost indescribable. This is not a dark, morbid off-with-your-head-if-you-do-not-obey type kingdom, but those in God's kingdom joyfully and peacefully do right!

> For the kingdom of God is not meat and drink; but righteousness, and peace, and joy in the Holy Ghost. For he that in these things serveth Christ is acceptable to God, and approved of men. (Rom. 14:17–18)

Search for areas in your own life where God has been dethroned and you have taken over His throne. Every worry, every fear, every satisfied lust, every outburst of anger reveals the secret hideouts (mini-kingdoms) you have been holding on to and keeping away from God's sovereign control.

- What is in your mini-kingdom that God would never allow in His kingdom?
- What is your number one motivator in life?
- Why do you do what you do every day?
- Why do you or do you not communicate with your King on a daily basis?

"All these things." What things? What you eat. What you drink. What you wear. The things that most people run after. We naturally want to be feeling good and looking good. Man was not made to be miserable. He naturally wants to be happy, even though he gets confused about what may bring true happiness. Please understand that every sin is simply a misguided attempt for happiness. Why would anyone want to be hungry or look ugly? It is when the feel-good-look-good motivator of life takes over and we focus on the temporal here and now and forget the eternal God and forever that our priorities become our loves and we fall into the common-man trap of loving and serving the creature more than the Creator. So what is your number one priority in life? You? God? A refusal to live in God's kingdom under His authority is a stressful way to live.

Simply stated by Jesus Himself, seek first what is important to God, and He will take care of everything you need. You can prioritize stress right out of your life.

Meditation 26

Live one day at a time.

This is what God says.

Matthew 6:34

Take therefore no thought for the morrow: for the morrow shall take thought for the things of itself. Sufficient unto the day is the evil thereof.

How can this affect me?

"Therefore." Because your heavenly Father knows what you need and promises to take care of you, don't worry about what might happen tomorrow; don't stress over future problems; don't fret over the worst possible scenarios, because tomorrow is tomorrow, and you will face its troubles when tomorrow comes. There are enough troubling problems to sufficiently fill today that you don't need to borrow from tomorrow. Live one day at a time.

Focusing on today helps us enjoy the pleasures God has given today without distraction. It is hard to think about two things at the same time and give both one hundred percent attention.

Fear is stressful. Fear of the future sits on the window sill of your soul looking for opportunities to deceive you by distorting reality (what is) into extreme negative possibilities (what could be, but seldom is).

The fear of rejection tells you that you will never be accepted or popular if you don't give up your "holy" lifestyle. The fear of discomfort lies in telling you that all the comfort you now enjoy will disappear in a breath if you do not seek and hoard more stuff. The fear of loneliness makes you believe that you will never enjoy sensual pleasures with a life mate if you don't give in to physical involvement before marriage. Such fear will rob you of future acceptance, contentment, and satisfying love and replace these joys with compromise, greed, and lust.

Fear lies. Fear deceives. Fear refuses to trust God's Word, God's will, and God's timing by creating a mistrust in God's ability to take care of us. Fear denies that God eagerly and graciously offers real love, real joy, and real peace.

The Bible is full of encouraging passages that remind us of God's daily protection and provision. No one wants to be enslaved by the *what ifs* of tomorrow when they can enjoy *what is* today. Here are two simple principles that will reduce stressful worry and anxiety.

Focus on Morning Mercies

Remind yourself that the day you are enjoying (right now, today, this very moment as you read this book) you do not deserve and is a gift from God. Don't assume that you will even live another day. Every day that we live and breathe is only possible because of God's marvelous mercies and loving compassion. How old are you? 14? 22? 58? 92? Simply multiply your age by 365, and you will see how many days God has already protected you and provided for you. Stressing out about what might happen tomorrow ignores hundreds of days of God's mercy in the past. What He has done yesterday He will continue to do tomorrow. It would do you well to memorize Lamentations 3:22–23.

It is of the Lord's mercies that we are not consumed, because his compassions fail not. They are new every morning: great is thy faithfulness.

Create a Manna Mindset

God promised to send manna every morning, and the manna *was* faithfully delivered new and fresh every morning. Everyone had just enough—not too much and not too little. No one had to worry about the next day's provision because God never missed a day. Every day God sent just enough for every person. For those who distrusted God's faithful provision and disobeyed God by taking enough manna for two days, there were distasteful consequences. Sneaking a bite of leftover manna resulted in a mouthful of worms and maggots. Think about the Lord's careful instruction regarding His daily provision of this manna.

> Then said the Lord unto Moses, Behold, I will rain bread from heaven for you; and the people shall go out and gather a certain rate [quota] every day, that I may prove [test] them, whether they will walk in my law, or no. And it shall come to pass, that on the sixth day they shall prepare that which they bring in; and it shall be twice as much as they gather daily." (Ex. 16:4–5)

So it was that quail came up at evening and covered the camp, and in the morning the dew lay all around the camp. And when the layer of dew lifted, there, on the surface of the wilderness, was a small round substance, as fine as frost on the ground. So when the children of Israel saw it, they said to one another, "What is it?" For they did not know what it was.

And Moses said to them, "This is the bread which the Lord has given you to eat. This is the thing which the Lord has commanded: 'Let every man gather it according to each one's need, one omer for each person, according to the number of persons; let every man take for those who are in his tent.'"

Then the children of Israel did so and gathered, some more, some less. So when they measured it by omers, he who gathered much had nothing left over, and he who gathered little had no lack. Every man had gathered according to each one's need. And Moses said, "Let no one leave any of it till morning." Notwithstanding they did not heed Moses. But some of them left part of it until morning, and it bred worms and stank. And Moses was angry with them. So they gathered it every morning, every man according to his need. And when the sun became hot, it melted. (Ex. 16:13–21 NKJV)

God promises strength for today. And He will empower you again tomorrow for tomorrow. He does not seem to give a week's strength all at one time. If you only have a day's ration of strength today, use it fully and don't think you'll run out. God will provide more strength tomorrow to handle tomorrow's heavy burdens. Believe it! Your faith in God's daily provision pleases Him. Your assurance in God's daily protection keeps you dependent on Him. When you believe He will be there for you every day, He is pleased and your stress will disappear—one day at a time.

When you learn to cherish today, to appreciate now, and to be thankful for each breath God gives you, you will see your stress lessen and your trust increase.

Meditation 27

Work on changing yourself— not everyone else.

This is what God says.

Matthew 7:1–6

Judge not, that ye be not judged. For with what judgment ye judge, ye shall be judged: and with what measure ye mete, it shall be measured to you again. And why beholdest thou the mote [speck] that is in thy brother's eye, but considerest not the beam [log] that is in thine own eye? Or how wilt thou say to thy brother, Let me pull out the mote [speck] out of thine eye; and, behold, a beam [log] is in thine own eye? Thou hypocrite, first cast out the beam [log] out of thine own eye; and then shalt thou see clearly to cast out the mote [speck] out of thy brother's eye. Give not that which is holy unto the dogs, neither cast ye your pearls before swine, lest they trample them under their feet, and turn again and rend you [tear you in pieces].

How can this affect me?

If you want to keep your stress level on high alert, live every day with a judgmental, critical spirit. A critical person gets stressed when others don't follow their preferences and assumed convictions. We get stressed when we believe that others think poorly of us, criticize us, and recruit former friends to join their critical team. Whether we are constantly criticizing others or others are constantly criticizing us, we will be stressed.

Timing is everything. Wouldn't it be nice if the negative, spiritual loggers who are just waiting for a chance to prejudge or criticize others would give others time to do some self-inspection? You see, a calm mind controlled by the Spirit of God can creatively solve life's issues and accomplish great things. If you catch yourself constantly criticizing others, try to give those growing in grace the same patience that God has given you.

If you hurry them, nag them, or distract them before they can solve their own problems, you are robbing them of spiritual discernment. If you disagree with them before they disagree with themselves, judge them before they have judged themselves, criticize them before they have had the calmness of mind to critique themselves, they will never fix what is broken. Don't try to be the Holy Spirit in other people's lives. Give God's Holy Spirit time to do His work.

Why are we so blinded to our own problems and yet see the problems in others so clearly? Why is it easier to critique than to compliment? Why is it so much easier to blast others for their failures rather than encourage others when they are being used by God to impact lives for Christ?

Be careful. We should not prejudge any man. Why? We seldom know all the facts or the heart of the person. No man knows the strength of another man's temptations. Those coming from great homes do not understand the struggles of those from dysfunctional backgrounds. Those from difficult homes do not understand those who are raised in godly homes. It is almost impossible for any of us to be impartial in our judgment. We think everyone looks at life through our own eyes. Only God knows heart motives. When we judge a man's motives, we are pretending to be omniscient. Be careful. Omniscience is an attribute that belongs only to God—not to us.

Work on changing yourself before you go after others. You hardly know your own heart. Do you know why you do what you do? Have you ever analyzed what motivates your life? Judge yourself. Critique your own heart. Analyze your own daily decisions. Get real close to the mirror of God's Word and search for the logs and the specks in your own eyes.

Preaching the gospel to yourself changes the way you view others. At the foot of the cross, as wretched sinners, all of us are on equal footing. No one deserves God's mercies. God loves and pities us as weak, impulsive, angry, lazy, moody, controlling, and stubborn children. If we could just look at others the same way that God looks at us, we would not stress over the imperfections and inconsistencies in others. We would stress less.

Work on changing yourself—not everyone else.

Meditation 28

Don't be afraid to ask for help.

This is what God says.

Matthew 7:7–11

Ask, and it shall be given you; seek, and ye shall find; knock, and it shall be opened unto you: For every one that asketh receiveth; and he that seeketh findeth; and to him that knocketh it shall be opened. Or what man is there of you, whom if his son ask bread, will he give him a stone? Or if he ask a fish, will he give him a serpent? If ye then, being evil, know how to give good gifts unto your children, how much more shall your Father which is in heaven give good things to them that ask Him?

How can this affect me?

It is commonly known that there are some men who refuse to ask for directions. They just get stressed when they are lost and more stressed when they cannot figure out how to hook up their latest electronic gadget.

Asking for help does not express weakness; it demonstrates wisdom.

The Lord reminds us that we can do nothing in ourselves but can do great things through Him. How often do you ask God for strength? How intensely do you seek God's power? How persevering are you in knocking on the door for God to answer?

As Jesus' sermon comes to an end (and our 31-day meditation study comes to a close), Jesus gives a hint on how we can live what we have learned without stressing over constant defeat and failure. Don't fear. Don't worry. Don't stress. Ask. Seek. Knock.

Ask and keep asking until you receive it. Seek and keep seeking until you find it. Knock and keep knocking until the door is opened. Notice the rise in intensity. Ask from a humble heart viewing yourself as a desperate inferior asking a kind superior. Seek by asking plus acting, and keep seeking until you find it. Knocking is asking plus acting plus persevering. Keep knocking until the door is opened.

Without the grace of God, we will never develop the character or life attitude that was described in the Beatitudes of Matthew 5:3–13. We need to ask, seek, and knock for God's grace.

Without the power of God, we will never be the kind of salt that creates a thirst for God in others or the light that draws men to our Savior (Matt. 5:13–14). We need to ask, seek, and knock for God's power.

Without the strength that God offers, we will never protect ourselves from the heart sins of anger, lust, and greed (Matt. 5:21–32; 6:1–4). We need to ask, seek, and knock for God's strength.

Without the enablement that God promises, we will never learn to love others, even our enemies, in a way that truly honors God (Matt. 5:38–48). We need to ask, seek, and knock for God's divine enablement.

Without the wisdom of God, we will never learn to pray in a fervent and effectual way (Matt. 6:5–13). We need to ask, seek, and knock for God's wisdom.

Without trusting in the provision of God, we will worry and never learn to depend on Him and Him alone (Matt. 6:19–34). We need to ask, seek, and knock for God's daily provision.

Without an understanding of God's Word, we will never learn the difference between critically judging others and biblical discernment (Matt. 7:1–6). We need to ask, seek, and knock for God's understanding.

Instead of giving in to failure, ask, seek, and knock.

> I am the vine, ye are the branches: He that abideth in me, and I in him, the same bringeth forth much fruit: for without me ye can do thing. (John 15:5)

Instead of being consumed with fear, ask, seek, and knock.

> Fear thou not; for I am with thee: be not dismayed; for I am thy God: I will strengthen thee; yea, I will help thee; yea, I will uphold thee with the right hand of My righteousness. (Isa. 41:10)

Instead of being devastated with weakness, ask, seek, and knock.

> Finally, my brethren, be strong in the Lord, and in the power of His might. (Eph. 6:10)

Instead of struggling in any way, ask, seek, and knock.

> That ye might walk worthy of the Lord unto all pleasing, being fruitful in every good work, and increasing in the knowledge of God; Strengthened with all might, according to His glorious power, unto all patience and longsuffering with joyfulness. (Col. 1:10–11)

And God will never disappoint us! He only gives good gifts. He will never throw stones at us. No snakes will slither up and strike us. God only gives good things. But we need to pray. We need to ask until it is given. We need to seek until we find. We need to knock until God opens the door.

The Heavenly Father loves His children and takes care of them, but He wants them to ask for the things they need, not just to help them determine the difference between necessities and niceties, but to acknowledge their dependence on Him.

God always answers. Sometimes "yes." Sometimes "no." Sometimes "wait." God will not disappoint His children. He may not give us what we ask, but He will never give us anything that is bad for us.

Remember Matthew 7:9, which says, "What man is there of you, whom if his son *ask* bread, will he give him a stone? Or if he *ask* a fish, will he give him a serpent? If ye then, being evil, know how to give good gifts unto your children, how much more shall your Father which is in heaven give good things to them that *ask* him?"

Notice how many times the word *ask* is emphasized? God is waiting for you to *ask*. God is wanting you to *ask*. God is willing to give to those who *ask*. What needs to change in your life in the way that you ask God for strength, seek God for wisdom, and persevere by knocking until you receive what you ask for?

> Call unto me, and I will answer thee, and shew thee great and mighty things, which thou knowest not. (Jer. 33:3)

Meditation 29

Practice the Golden Rule.

This is what God says.

Matthew 7:12

Therefore all things whatsoever ye would that men should do to you, do ye even so to them: for this is the law and the prophets.

How can this affect me?

"Do unto others as you would have them do unto you." In everything, therefore, treat people the same way you want them to treat you. This sums up all that is taught in the Law and the Prophets.

Do you feel that you are treated unfairly by anyone? Do you complain because you have very few friends and wonder why no one ever visits you? What do you think about most: what others do for you or what you do for others? Does believing that nobody cares about you bother you? Stress you?

The Golden Rule is taken from a Bible principle that has been reworded, rephrased, and refocused by almost every religion and every generation in history. Too often it has been taken from its negative side rather than its positive side. In other words, if you don't want your sister to hit you, don't hit her! If you don't want to be treated like a child, don't treat others that way. If you don't want to be laughed at, don't laugh at others. It is the don't-and-they-won't approach to life.

Our Lord emphasizes the *do* and not the *don't*. Why *do*? *Do* sets an example. *Do* establishes a pattern. *Do* gives hope that it can be done! If you want others to be kind and not hateful to you, what should you *do*? If you want others to treat you and your purity with respect, what should you *do*? If you want others to be honest, go the extra mile, and turn the other cheek, what should you *do*? How can you *do* kindness? How can you *do* forgiveness? How can you *do* patience? How can you *do* Christlike love?

Make sure that your expectations are mirrored by your example. There are some who may have never learned how to *do* kindness, patience, forgiveness, and love. There are some who have never even seen a loving, godly family. For some, our *doing* is the only instruction manual they will ever read. Don't wait for others to *do* to you, you *do* first and watch them follow your example.

Why do you think Jesus compared this Golden Rule with "the law and the prophets"? How is treating others like you want them to treat you fulfilling Scripture? When Jesus was asked by the lawyer in Matthew 22:36–37 which commandment was the most important, He replied, "Thou shalt love the Lord thy God with all thy heart, and with all thy soul, and with all thy mind. This is the first and great commandment. And the second is like unto it, Thou shalt love thy neighbor as thyself." Then in Matthew 22:40 Jesus repeated what He taught on the Galilean hillside with this Golden Rule as He said, "On these two commandments hang all the law and the prophets."

So loving God and loving others fulfills God's law. Such love involves *doing*. It is care, compassion, and consideration with work gloves on. It is getting dirty as you dig into the lives of hurting people. In the past six months, who have you served, encouraged, or helped?

Don't love like you have been loved or expect to be loved, but love like you *want* to be loved.

This principle is short enough to memorize, simple enough to understand, and specific enough to do. Commentator Arthur Pink explains, "Its very brevity evidences the Divine wisdom of Him who spoke as never man spoke, for who else could have condensed so much into so few words."[1] J. C. Ryle says of the Golden Rule, "It settles a hundred difficult points, which in a world like this are continually arising between man and man. It prevents the necessity of laying down endless little rules for our conduct in specific cases."[2]

Do you want to obey what Christ calls the greatest of all commandments, impact others, and reduce the inner stress that often controls your heart?

"Do unto others as you would have them do unto you."

Meditation 30

Beware of wolves.

This is what God says.
Matthew 7:13–23

Enter ye in at the strait gate: for wide is the gate, and broad is the way, that leadeth to destruction, and many there be which go in thereat: because strait is the gate, and narrow is the way, which leadeth unto life, and few there be that find it. Beware of false prophets, which come to you in sheep's clothing, but inwardly they are ravening wolves. Ye shall know them by their fruits. Do men gather grapes of thorns, or figs of thistles? Even so every good tree bringeth forth good fruit; but a corrupt tree bringeth forth evil fruit. A good tree cannot bring forth evil fruit, neither can a corrupt tree bring forth good fruit. Every tree that bringeth not forth good fruit is hewn down, and cast into the fire. Wherefore by their fruits ye shall know them. Not everyone that saith unto me, Lord, Lord, shall enter into the kingdom of heaven; but he that doeth the will of my

Father which is in heaven. Many will say to me in that day, Lord, Lord, have we not prophesied in thy name? And in thy name have cast out devils? And in thy name done many wonderful works? And then will I profess unto them, I never knew you: depart from me, ye that work iniquity.

How can this affect me?

Confusion equals stress. Doubts can cause anxiety. If someone is constantly attempting to attack or discredit what or who you are trusting in, you might get a bit worried. Satan is the king of twisting, turning, and perverting the truth in order to get God's children to doubt what God has said (Gen. 3:1–5; Gal. 1:7–8; Acts 13:9–10).

Beware of wolves who seek to pollute the purity of the gospel. Beware of spiritual thieves who attempt to rob people of the simplicity of the gospel message. Beware of anyone who teaches that you can "make it" to heaven by good works, by giving lots of money, by being generous to the poor, or by doing the best that you can. Beware of any wolf-like leaders who teach that there is any way to God other than through the death, burial, and resurrection of Jesus Christ.

Jesus Christ, the very Son of God, came to earth, lived a sinless life, was crucified on a cruel cross for our sins, was buried, rose from the dead, ascended to heaven, and will return for all those who have trusted in Him.

Beware of wolves (false teachers) who teach any other gospel than the simple, pure gospel of Jesus Christ. Beware of wolves (deceiving religious leaders) who deny that we are all sinners in need of a Savior who can forgive and separate our sins from us so we will never be separated from God. Constantly be on guard against false teachers who twist, turn, and pervert Scripture to say what they want to say (so they can do what they want to do). Beware of heretical teachers who come to you disguised as harmless sheep, but inwardly, are vicious, ferocious, ravenous wolves who desire to tear you apart and keep you as far from God as they possibly can.

Beware. Be careful. Be cautious. Be wary. Watch out. Think twice. Keep your eyes peeled. Be on the lookout. Be alert to the potential dangers ahead.

Beware of the kind of wolves that love deception. Wolves distract the sheep in order to get their eyes off the shepherd so they can easily be led astray. Beware of wolves that love disunity. Wolves scatter the sheep so they can attack them one at a time. Beware of wolves that love disloyalty. Wolves drive the sheep as far from the shepherd as they can so they can destroy them without resistance. Beware of wolves that love division. Wolves love to divide and conquer. Beware of wolves.

Wolves are false prophets, or as we know them today, heretical teachers who have no "strait gate" and "narrow way" in their gospel message. They completely overlook sin. There is no offense of the cross, no burden to bear, no unpopular positions to take. They teach a false gospel based on what men can do rather than what Christ has done.

Some wolves look just like sheep. It is not what they say, but what they don't say that is so dangerous. What popular religious systems in our world emphasize good works and religious traditions but deny the fact that Jesus Christ is the only way to heaven? What kind of teaching emphasizes extreme preferences as truth and distracts us from our walk with God and desire to introduce our friends to our wonderful Lord? What is being taught from our pulpits and argued from our pews that causes great division, ultimately scattering the sheep in every direction, destroying the unity of the flock, and distracting us from making disciples?

Any stress that we have dealt with in our few, short years of this life will pale in comparison with the stress of hearing what I consider some of the saddest words in all of Scripture: "I never knew you: depart from me" (Matt. 7:23).

God will speak these words to those who try to defend themselves by crying, "Lord, Lord, look what we have done!" God does not just examine the externals (what we have done), but searches the heart (who we are in Christ). The pharisaical white and wooly wolves would get an "A" on the externals, but they will fail the heart-search. A careful inspection of our own hearts reveals who or what we are trusting in for the forgiveness of our sins as well as what we do for Christ or what He has done for us.

Man must believe that Jesus Christ died, was buried, and rose from the dead. Sin's penalty is death. Jesus never sinned. He died for your sin and my sin. He conquered death and rose from the grave, thus making a way that our sins could be forever forgiven, thus enabling us to enter into God's presence in heaven someday.

If you are constantly stressed over the assurance of your salvation, could it be that you are unknowingly being beguiled by a deceitful wolf? Are you entertaining any teaching or philosophy that contradicts the Word of God? Are you challenging the simple truth of the gospel? Are you doubting the very Word of God? If so, look around. I promise there is a wolf close by.

Meditation 31

Sing "The wise man built his house upon a rock!"

This is what God says.

Matthew 7:24–29

Therefore whosoever heareth these sayings of mine, and doeth them, I will liken him unto a wise man, which built his house upon a rock: and the rain descended, and the floods came, and the winds blew, and beat upon that house; and it fell not: for it was founded upon a rock. And every one that heareth these sayings of mine, and doeth them not, shall be likened unto a foolish man, which built his house upon the sand: and the rain descended, and the floods came, and the winds blew, and beat upon that house; and it fell: and great was the fall of it. And it came to pass, when Jesus had ended these sayings, the people were astonished at his doctrine: for he taught them as one having authority, and not as the scribes.

How can this affect me?

Here is our Lord's final, foundational principle that most three-year-old kids sing about and numbers of many-year-olds forget.

Stressful times will come. The storms will huff, and puff, and attempt to blow our houses down! The storms of life actually become spiritual building inspectors. They reveal to us what kind of foundation we are building our lives on. Before any of us think that we have unique problems unlike anyone else on earth, we had better recognize that the Lord describes only two builders: not three, four, or five. Just two.

What is the difference between the secure wise man and the stressed-out foolish man? Both built a house; they had to live. Both experienced the storms of life complete with violent winds, torrential rains, and devastating floods. Both heard what God said ("the sayings of mine [the Lord]"). Both had a choice to obey ("and doeth them") or to disobey ("and doeth them not").

The difference was that the wise man prepared for the stressful storms of life, knowing that one day they would come. The foolish man took the easy way out, thinking that the bright and sunny days would always be there.

The difference was one obeyed God and the other did not. The secure wise man's house did not fall; the stressed-out foolish man's had a great fall.

Summer suns do not shine forever. Days of storms and stress, of sweeping winds and whistling, howling rains will come. Look at the two houses. What is happening? One of them, under the pressure of the storm, is crumbling and falling. The man is rendered homeless. The other house is standing erect, firm, and strong. The man is safe and secure. What made the difference? Simple obedience. Simply trusting and obeying what Christ said.

We have just spent thirty-one days meditating on Christ's life-changing Sermon on the Mount. Reread this meditation. Remind yourself of Christ's blessed instruction. Don't put this little book on a shelf until its teachings are part of your heart and soul.

I love the way our Lord finishes His message. Life is a choice. Stress is a choice. Trust is a choice. God is God. His omnipotence, omniscience, omnipresence, and never-ending love make Him the only truly trustworthy being in the entire universe.

What the Son of God told His listeners, God the Father told Joshua many years before, and the Spirit of God is telling us today many years later.

> This book of the law shall not depart out of thy mouth; but thou shalt meditate therein day and night, that thou mayest observe to do according to all that is written therein; for then thou shalt make thy way prosperous, and then thou shalt have good success. (Josh. 1:8)

"Trust and obey, for there's no other way, to be happy [stress-free] in Jesus, but to trust and obey.[1]

Epilogue

Matthew 7:28–29

And it came to pass, when Jesus had ended these sayings, the people were astonished at his doctrine: for he [Jesus] taught them as one having authority, and not as the scribes.

We too should be astonished at our Lord's authority. He is the ultimate authority because of His *knowledge*. He knows all.

He is the ultimate authority because of His *life*. He lived without sin and never violated one of these principles.

He is the ultimate authority because of His *love*. When a person says something out of love, we normally listen. Everything Jesus taught is for our good. No selfish agendas. No personal gain.

He is the ultimate authority. We should be astonished. Amazed. And so thankful that we can call Him our loving, heavenly Father.

Stress less. Trust more.

Notes

Too Blessed to Be Stressed
1. Megan Kaye, *Stress: The Psychology of Managing Pressure* (New York: DK Publishing, 2017), 12.

Meditation 4
1. A. W. Pink, *Studies in the Scriptures, 1937 (Jul.–Dec.)–1938* (Lafayette, IN: Sovereign Grace Publishers, Inc., 2005), 9:291.

Meditation 10
1. "Jefferson's Salt Mountain," http://historyrfd.net/isern/103/salt.htm.

2. "The Many Uses of Salt," www.maldonsalt.co.uk/About-Salt-The-many-uses-of-Salt.html.

Meditation 16
1. John F. MacArthur, *The MacArthur New Testament Commentary: Matthew 1–7* (Chicago: Moody Press, 1985), 354.

Meditation 17
1. *The MacArthur New Testament Commentary*, 393.

Meditation 21

1. Charles Haddon Spurgeon, *Morning and Evening: Daily Readings*, "Morning, May 26," Christian Classics Ethereal Library, http://www.ccel.org/ccel/spurgeon/morneve.html.

Meditation 22

1. William Hendriksen and Simon J. Kistemaker, *New Testament Commentary: Exposition of the Gospel According to Matthew* (Grand Rapids: Baker Books, 1976), 351.

Meditation 23

1. Elizabeth George, *Breaking the Worry Habit . . . Forever* (Eugene, OR: Harvest House Publishers, 2009), 20.

2. Reinhold Niebuhr, "The Serenity Prayer," http://www.beliefnet.com/prayers/protestant/addiction/serenity-prayer.aspx.

Meditation 29

1. Arthur W. Pink, *Sermon on the Mount* (Lafayette, IN: Sovereign Grace Publishers, Inc., 2002), 316.

2. J. C. Ryle, *Expository Thoughts on the Gospels* (New York: Robert Carter & Brothers, 1860), 66.)

Meditation 31

1. John H. Sammis, "Trust and Obey," 1887.